Quick-Sew FLEECE

Fast & Fun Fleece For All Seasons
From America's Top Designers

QUICK-SEW FLEECE

Copyright © 1998 by Landauer Corporation

This book was designed and produced by Landauer Books
A division of Landauer Corporation
12251 Maffitt Road, Cumming, Iowa 50061

President: Jeramy Lanigan Landauer
Vice President: Becky Johnston
Managing Editor: Marlene Hemberger Heuertz
Project Editor: Mary V. Green
Creative Director: Margaret Sindelar
Art Director: Robert Mickey Hager
Graphic Design: Karla Kuhn
Cover Design: Tracy DeVenney
Cover Photo: Amy Cooper
Associate Editor: Sarah Reid
Copy Editor: Linda Delbridge-Parker
Technical Illustrator: Stan Green/Green Graphics
Graphics Technician: Stewart Cott
Creative Assistant: Laurel Albright
Photographers: Craig Anderson, Amy Cooper, and Dennis Kennedy

Published by Martingale & Company
PO Box 118, Bothell, WA 98041-0118 USA

Library of Congress Cataloging-in-Publication Data

Quick-sew fleece: fast & fun fleece for all seasons from America's top designers/editor Becky Johnston.
    p. cm. —(Best-loved designers collection)
  Includes index.
  ISBN 1-56477-231-4 (softcover)
  1. Sewing. 2. Handicraft. 3. Synthetic fabrics. I. Johnston, Becky. II. Series.
  TT715.Q53 1998
  646.2—dc21   98-28575
                                                      CIP

Printed in Hong Kong on acid-free paper.

10 9 8 7 6 5 4 3 2 1

BEST–LOVED DESIGNERS
C O L L E C T I O N

Quick-Sew
FLEECE

Fast & Fun Fleece For All Seasons
From America's Top Designers

Edited by Becky Johnston

Cozy Hat, Mittens, and Scarf pg. 11

Fishies and Froggies Beach Set pg. 26

Panda Pals pg. 36

Babushka Dolls pg. 48

TABLE OF CONTENTS

Crossover Vest   pg. 60

Halloween Checkers Set   pg. 66

Sunflower Bag   pg. 84

Adorable Hats   pg. 110

Sailboat Tote   pg. 94

Kari Pearson
K.P. Kids & Company

Cheryl Jukich
Threadbare Pattern Company

Margaret Sindelar
Cottonwood Classics

Janet Carija Brandt
Carijarts

Nancy Cornwell
Stretch & Sew Fabrics®

Judith Carter & Leigh Anne Roach
Custom Threads.

Merry Nader
Merry Nader's Designs

Janet Bullis
Creative Services

Mary Mulari
Mary's Productions

INTRODUCTION

Back by popular demand, America's Best-Loved Designers bring you the best and brightest of the newest fabric trend—fleece! Discover four seasons of fun with fleece when you go beyond the familiar warm-as-toast Polar Fleece® to the cozy blanket fleece and the buttery soft microfleece, just right for spring and summer.

To get you started, each of the leading fabric artisans has designed an exciting new collection of fast and fun fleece projects to take you through the seasons, including a colorful spring jacket, autumn leaves on a fleece blanket in a complementary bag, and kids' drawings on a fleece-bordered pillow and coordinated tote for summertime fun. For a special event or a last-minute gift, make-it-quick with fresh new inspirations for everything from green and red holiday outfits for the popular stuffed beanbag toys to a trio of whimsical "sand bucket"-inspired fleece gift bags to fill with birthday treats, or sunglasses, sunscreen, and a paperback novel for a mini-beach party! For fleece with a flair, top it all off with an elegant holiday muff, hat, and scarf.

Each chapter is devoted to one of the nine contributing designers and includes imaginative featured projects such as pillows, wearables, tote bags, decorative accessories, gifts, and embellished accents for your home.

Best of all, the projects are quick, easy, and fun to make—four seasons of fleece to finish in a flash and enjoy throughout the year!

Becky Johnston
Editor

Kari Pearson

K. P. KIDS AND COMPANY

What could be cuter than cherubic little children all decked out in fleece finery from award-winning K. P. Kids and Company?

Designer Kari Pearson has turned her magic in designing kids' fashions and fabrics to fleece—and the results are accessories no child will want to be without!

While big kids are getting ready to prowl the neighborhood in scary costumes, the little ones can look just as cute in the seasonal Kitty Vest, accented by the sweet little Pumpkin Pouch to carry a handful of candy corn kernels You can also adapt the pumpkin into pin.

When the seasons change and it's time for the first snowman, your child will stay warm and toasty in the Cozy Hat, Mittens and Scarf set all winter long, since the inside is just as soft and fuzzy as the outside, with its colorful plaid flannel lining.

Of course, spring is always around the corner, and what better way to celebrate than with a game of I Love Spring Bean Bag Toss or Hopscotch. For Valentine's Day, a special birthday, or just to say, "Hooray, spring is here!" you'll find lots of reasons to whip up quick and easy scalloped heart bean bags.

For the special little girl in your life, make her summer just as special, with a delightful Sunflower Satchel or the Posey Purse—one for the beach and one for Sunday best! Top everything off with smaller motifs for a pin or to trim her straw hat!

MATERIALS

- Purchased pattern for child's vest (I used K.P. Kids Pattern number 1014)
- ½ yard of black fleece for vest
- ½ yard of plaid flannel for lining
- One 9" x 12" piece of medium-gray felt for appliqués
- Scraps of light gray, white, black, and assorted bright colored felt (orange, green, red, yellow, pink, purple) for appliqués
- 4" x 8" piece of orange fleece
- 30" black rattail cording
- Black and orange embroidery floss
- Thread to match assorted felts
- Pattern tracing material
- Water-soluble glue stick

CUTTING

1. From the purchased vest pattern cut out two fronts and one back from the fleece and two fronts and one back from the flannel lining.
2. Using the patterns on pages 15-16, trace and cut out the following appliqués: from medium-gray felt, cut two cat faces; from light-gray felt, cut four ears and four cheeks; from white felt, cut two eye

SUMMER

WINTER

AUTUMN

SPRING

triangles and two eye circles; from black felt, cut two noses and four small eyes; and from the assorted bright colors, cut six stars, two bows, and one collar.

KITTY VEST ASSEMBLY

1. Use a ½" seam allowance throughout. With right sides together, stitch the vest front to the vest back at the shoulder seams. Finger press the seams open. Repeat for the vest lining fronts and back. Press the seams open.

2. Press under a ½" seam allowance on the side seams of the lining front and back. Then, with right sides together, pin the vest front and back to the lining front and back.

3. Stitch the vest to the lining along the bottom, front and back neck, and armholes. Leave the side seams open. See Diagram A. Trim seams, clip curves, and trim corners.

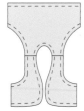

DIAGRAM A

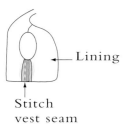

Stitch
vest seam
DIAGRAM B

4. Turn the vest right side out through one of the side openings, and finger press. With right sides together, pin the vest side seams together and stitch, as shown in Diagram B. Be careful not to catch the vest lining. Trim seams and finger press open. Hand-sew the lining closed at the side seams.

5. Using six strands of the orange embroidery floss, blanket-stitch around all edges of the vest by hand.

6. Assemble the cat appliqués before attaching them to the vest. Referring to the pattern for placement, dab the glue stick on the back of each cheek, eye, nose, and ear cutout. Stick them to the gray cat faces. Machine zigzag around each shape with thread that matches the appliqué piece. Add a touch of color to the ears and cheeks by dabbing a bit of powdered blush on them. Stitch mouth lines with a backstitch, and create whiskers by knotting floss and trimming the tails about 1" long.

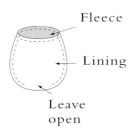

Fleece

Lining

Leave
open
DIAGRAM C

7. Pin the appliqués to the vest, referring to the photograph for placement. For the boy cat, zigzag stitch around the face, leaving the top of the head unsewn to create a pocket. Finish the boy cat by stitching the bowtie in place.

8. For the girl cat, stitch the collar in place first, followed by the cat face, and finish with the bow.

9. Zigzag stitch the stars in place with matching threads.

PUMPKIN POUCH ASSEMBLY

1. For the pumpkin pouch, cut two pumpkins from orange fleece and two from plaid flannel. Cut three leaves from green felt and two eyes and one nose from black felt.

2. Attach the eyes and nose to the right side of one of the pumpkin pieces using a zigzag stitch. Use a backstitch and black floss to hand-stitch the mouth, and orange floss and a running stitch to create the pumpkin lines.

3. To assemble the pumpkin, sew the two fleece pumpkin pieces, right sides together, along the curved edge only. Leave the top open. In the same way, sew the two flannel pumpkins right sides together, but leave a second opening at the bottom for turning.

4. Cut two pieces of rattail, each 15" long. Pin a rattail piece to each side seam of the pumpkin, so one end is flush with the top edge of the pumpkin pieces.

5. With right sides together, put the fleece pumpkin inside the flannel pumpkin, and stitch them together along the top edge. See Diagram C. Turn the pumpkin right side out through the opening in the lining. Hand-stitch the opening closed. Tie the rattail ends together to create a strap. Referring to the photograph, hand-stitch the leaves in place.

MATERIALS

- ¼ yard of turquoise Berber fleece

- ¼ yard of navy fleece

- 8" square or ¼ yard each of four coordinating colors of fleece

- 1¼ yards of plaid flannel

- 6" length of ⅛"-wide elastic

- Red, blue, green, and light green embroidery floss

- Thread to match Berber fleece

- Pattern tracing material

CUTTING

1. From the Berber fleece, cut one 6" x 20½" strip for the hat band, and four 1¾" x 6¾" strips for the scarf. Cut four mittens and one pom-pom circle using the patterns on pages 16-17.

2. From the flannel, cut eight mittens (four will be for interlining) and cut four hat sections on the fold. Cut four ties, each 1¼" x 7" and cut a 6¾" x 45" strip.

3. From the coordinating fleeces, cut two hat sections from each color, cutting along the outer line, not on the fold. Cut twelve 1¾"-squares each from two coordinating fleeces.

4. From the navy fleece, cut one 6¾" x 35" strip for the scarf. Cut 24 strips each ½" x 20" for fringe.

HAT ASSEMBLY

1. Use a ¼" seam allowance throughout. Sew the eight fleece hat sections together to form the crown of the hat. Match the straight edges of the sections and sew in pairs. Sew the resulting four sections together along the curved edges. See Diagram D. Repeat to sew the four flannel sections together for the lining.

2. Stitch the short ends of the band together. With the right side of the band facing the wrong side of the fleece hat, stitch the band to the hat.

3. Press under ¼" along the bottom edge of the flannel lining. Insert the flannel lining in the hat with wrong sides facing. Pin the lining in place along the bottom edge, so the pressed-under edge of the flannel overlaps the seam allowance where the band is stitched to the hat. Stitching through all layers, zigzag the flannel lining in place along the bottom edge.

4. Fold the band to the right side of the hat, folding up 2", then folding again.

5. By hand, gather the edge of the Berber fleece circle, as for a yo-yo. Pull taut and knot the thread. Attach the pom-pom, stitching through the hat and lining to secure.

MITTEN ASSEMBLY

1. Make a buttonhole in each Berber mitten where indicated on the pattern.

2. Cut two 1½" squares of dark blue fleece and embroider each with the tree pattern. Blanket-stitch the square in place on a left and right mitten.

3. With right sides together, sew two Berber mitten sections together, leaving the top edge open. Repeat for the other mitten.

4. Layer two flannel mitten pieces wrong sides together, and machine baste around the edges.

DIAGRAM D

Leave open

DIAGRAM E

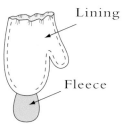

Lining

Fleece

DIAGRAM F

Repeat to make four pairs. Sew two flannel pairs together, leaving the top edge open as well as an opening at the tip of the fingers for turning. See Diagram E. Repeat with the other flannel pairs.

5. Place a Berber mitten inside a flannel mitten, right sides together. Stitch the sections together around the top opening. Turn the mitten right side out through the opening at the fingertips. See Diagram F. Hand-stitch the opening closed. Repeat for the other mitten.

6. Fold the flannel ties in half lengthwise, right sides together. Stitch the long edge with a ¼" seam allowance and turn right side out. Secure ties to each end of two 3" lengths of elastic.

7. Following the guideline on the mitten pattern, use embroidery floss and a running stitch to sew a casing on each mitten. Sew through all layers. Using a safety pin

or bodkin, insert a tie in a buttonhole and work it out through the other buttonhole. Tie a knot at each end of the tie to prevent raveling, then tie the ends together in a bow.

SCARF ASSEMBLY

1. You will need to make two checkerboard strips. For each, stitch six each of two coordinating fleece squares together, adding a Berber strip to each side. Sew a completed patchwork to each end of the navy fleece strip.

2. For fringe, evenly space six groups of two strips folded together along one end of scarf and baste in place. Repeat for other end. Right sides together, keeping fringe free, stitch flannel lining to scarf leaving an opening for turning. Turn right side out and stitch opening closed.

3. Knot fringe as desired.

Spring: I Love Spring Bean Bags

CUTTING

1. From assorted fleeces, cut six hearts using the pattern on page 18. Cut six contrasting rectangles, each 6½" x 8".

2. Cut six flowers from contrasting colors of fleece and 12 leaves from green fleece.

ASSEMBLY

1. Referring to the photograph for placement, hand-stitch the leaves and flowers in place on the hearts. To create a three-dimensional look, lightly gather the flat end of the leaves before attaching them. Sew a contrasting button through the center of each flower.

2. Sew each heart onto a contrasting fleece rectangle, stitching ⅛" from the edge of the heart. Leave an opening along a straight edge for filling. See Diagram G.

3. Turn the hearts over and use the pattern to trace scallops onto the backs of the bean bags. Cut out the scallops.

4. Fill the bean bags so they are three-dimensional, but not overstuffed. Topstitch the openings closed.

MATERIALS

- Assorted bright colored fleece scraps, at least 8" square
- Threads to match fleece colors
- Assorted buttons
- Pattern tracing material
- 2 bags of Polyfil pellets

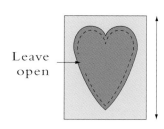

Leave open

DIAGRAM G

MATERIALS

- ¼ yard of blue cotton fabric for back and lining
- ⅛ yard of green cotton fabric for straps
- 8" square of green fleece
- 7" square of red fleece
- 4" square of pink fleece
- ¼ yard of medium to heavy-weight sew-in interfacing
- Red embroidery floss
- 1" strip of ½"-wide Velcro

CUTTING

1. From the blue cotton fabric, cut two purse backs and one purse front using the pattern on page 19. From the interfacing, cut one purse back and one front.
2. From the red fleece, cut one purse front.
3. From green fleece, cut four leaves. From pink fleece, cut one rose swirl. Cut the swirl apart on the spiral line.
4. From the green cotton fabric, cut two 1¼" x 15½" strips for handles.

ASSEMBLY

1. Fold the handle strips in half lengthwise. Stitch along the raw edges with a ¼" seam allowance. Turn right side out and press flat.

2. Machine baste the interfacing to the wrong side of one purse back. With raw edges even, pin the ends of one purse strap to the right side of the second purse back. Use the dots on the purse pattern as a guideline. See Diagram H.

3. With right sides together, sew the two purse back pieces together with a ¼" seam allowance, leaving about 2" open for turning. Turn right side out and press.

4. Pin the pink spiral to the right side of the red fleece purse front. Stitch in place by hand using 6 strands of red floss and a running stitch. Refer to the photograph for placement of the spiral.

5. Pin the remaining purse strap to the wrong side of the cotton purse front. Fold the flat ends of the leaves to form a pleat. Pin the leaves to the wrong side of the cotton purse front, referring to the photograph for placement.

6. Layer the fleece front and cotton front, wrong sides together. Pin the layered fronts to the purse back. Blanket-stitch through all layers by hand, starting at the leaves on one side, stitching around the bottom of the purse, and stopping at the leaves on the other side. Knot and clip the thread. Complete the blanket stitching by stitching the remainder of the purse front and back separately, so the purse has an opening.

7. Attach the Velcro tape to the inside of the purse front and back for a closure.

DIAGRAM H

CUTTING

1. From the yellow cotton fabric, cut two purse backs and one purse front using the pattern on page 19.
2. From the interfacing, cut one purse back. From the orange Berber fleece, cut one purse front.
3. From the yellow fleece, cut 14 large petals using the pattern on page 19. From rust fleece, cut 14 small petals.
4. From the green cotton fabric, cut one 1¼" x 44" strip for the handle.
5. From red or pink fleece scraps, cut two cheeks using the pattern on page 19.

MATERIALS

- ¼ yard of yellow cotton fabric
- ⅛ yard of green cotton fabric
- 7" square of orange Berber fleece
- 16" square of yellow fleece
- 16" square of rust fleece
- Scrap of red or pink fleece
- ¼ yard of medium to heavy-weight sew-in interfacing
- Black embroidery floss
- 1" piece of Velcro

ASSEMBLY

1. Assemble the purse back and turn it right side out following the directions for the Posey Purse, but omit attaching the strap.
2. For the purse front, first backstitch the sunflower face onto the Berber fleece, using six strands of black embroidery floss. Blanket-stitch the cheeks in place.
3. Fold the green strip in half lengthwise, right sides together, and stitch along the long edge using a ¼" seam allowance. Turn right side out and press flat.
4. Machine baste the purse front interfacing to the wrong side of the cotton purse front.
5. Fold a pleat in the flat edge of each rust petal and pin in place on the wrong side of the fleece purse front, spacing the petals apart evenly. See Diagram I.

Repeat for the yellow petals, centering them behind the rust petals. Insert the ends of the green strap between the petals and the sunflower, using the dots on the pattern as placement guides.

6. Layer the fleece sunflower over the wrong side of the cotton purse front. Pin the layered front sections to the purse back and pin together. Blanket-stitch by hand through all layers to assemble the purse, stitching only from one strap to the other and leaving the top open. Knot and clip the thread. Complete the blanket stitching by stitching the remainder of the purse front and back separately, so the purse has an opening.
7. Finish by sewing the Velcro pieces to the inside of the purse front and back. Adjust the strap length by tying a knot in the strap.

Wrong side

DIAGRAM I

PUMPKIN
POUCH PURSE

PUMPKIN
LEAF

BOW

COLLAR

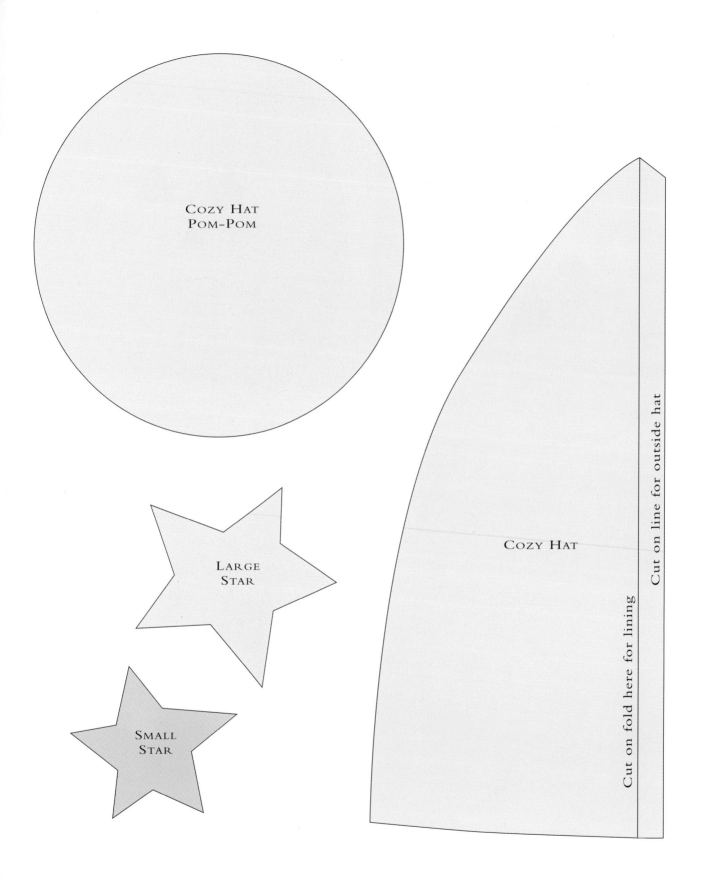

Cozy Hat
Pom-Pom

Large
Star

Small
Star

Cozy Hat

Cut on line for outside hat

Cut on fold here for lining

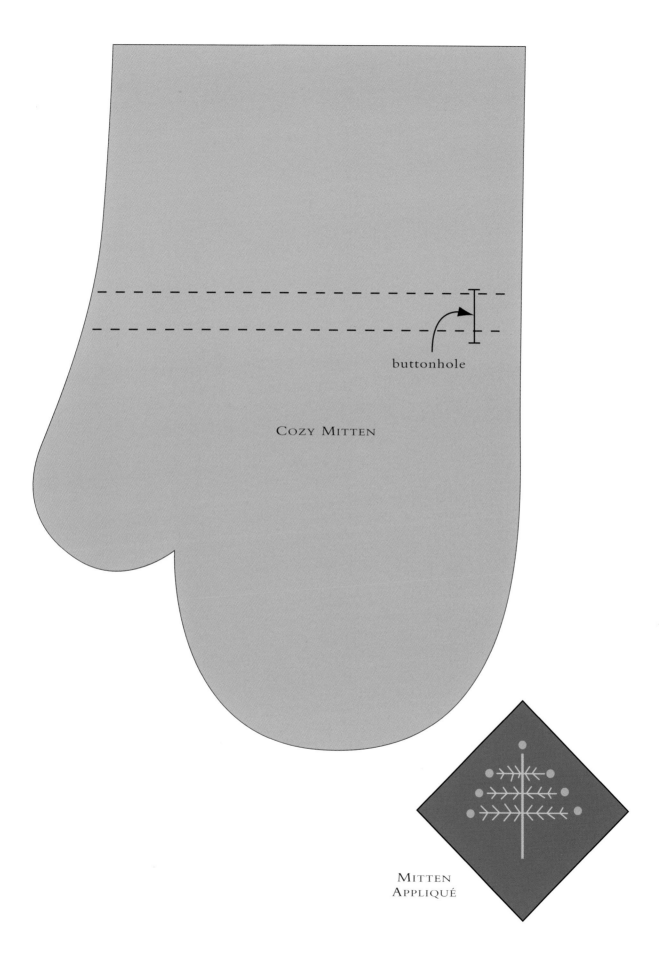

buttonhole

Cozy Mitten

Mitten
Appliqué

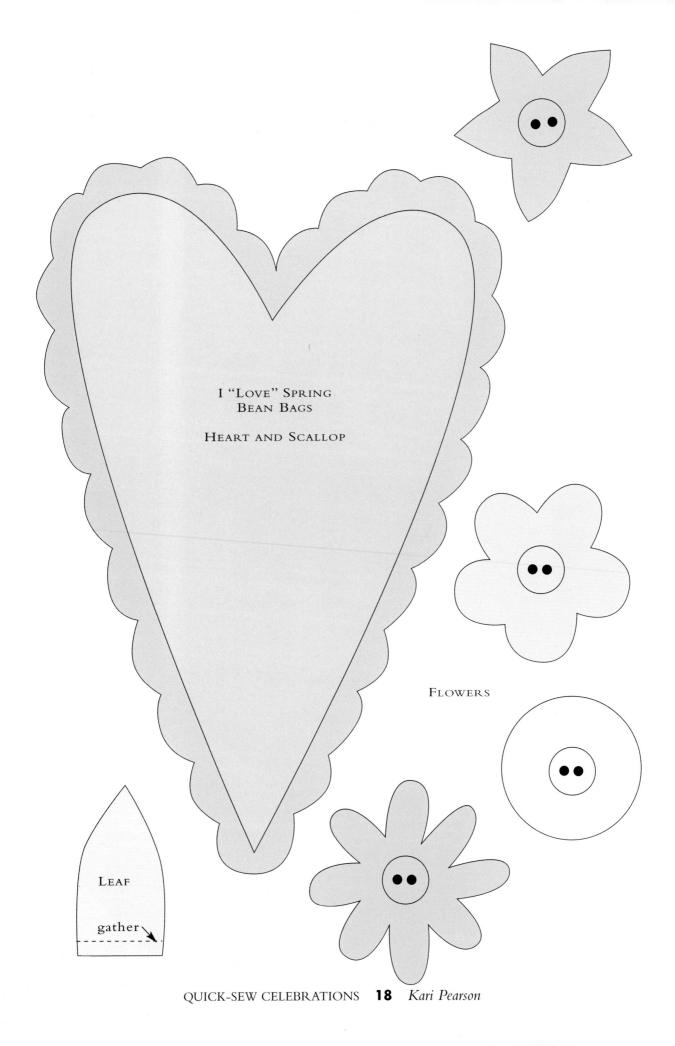

I "Love" Spring
Bean Bags

Heart and Scallop

Flowers

Leaf

gather

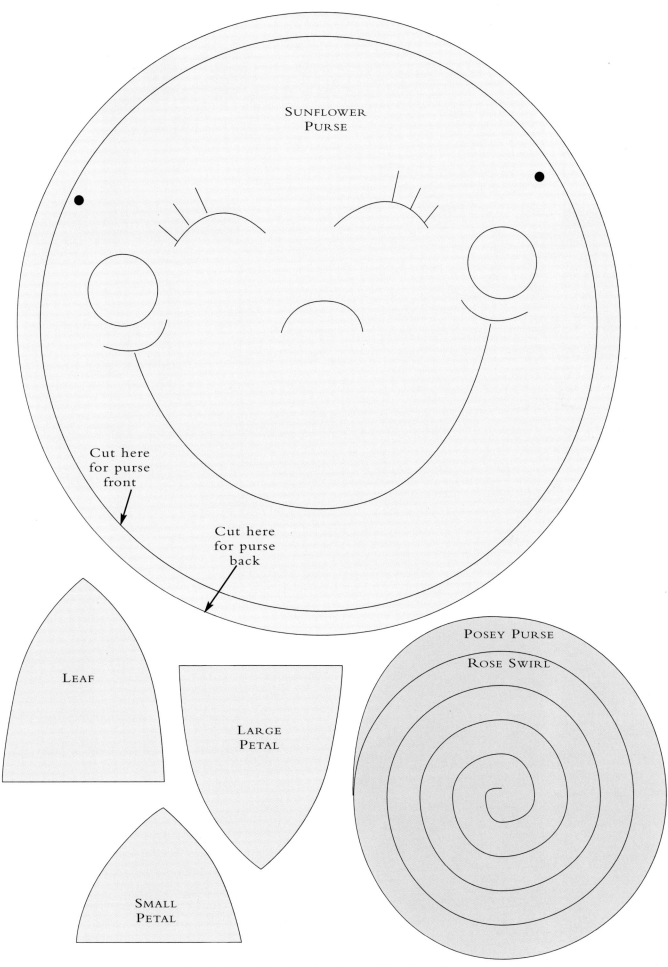

SUNFLOWER
PURSE

Cut here
for purse
front

Cut here
for purse
back

LEAF

LARGE
PETAL

SMALL
PETAL

POSEY PURSE

ROSE SWIRL

Cheryl Jukich

THREADBARE PATTERN COMPANY

Cheryl makes autumn fun with a bright and colorful back-to-school sweatshirt jacket. Her Quik-Quilt® technique turns an ordinary sweatshirt into something truly special.

What could be cozier on a cold winter evening than a good book, a mug of hot cocoa, and a big, comfy pillow to sink into! This oversized pillow is a snap to make since it starts with a purchased, two-sided blanket that's soft flannel on one side and cozy fleece on the other.

The coming of spring means bright, colorful flowers blooming everywhere, including those on the front of the pretty tulip jacket. This lightweight, cuddly topper will be the talk of the Easter egg hunt.

And for summer outings to the beach or the local park, how about a soft, lightweight fleece blanket. Clever fleece frogs filled with beans anchor the corners of the blanket on breezy days, and double as bean bag toys. Pack the blanket, the frogs, and lots of other essentials into the coordinating tote, and you're ready for a day of fun!

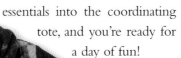

Autumn: Color Me Cozy Sweatshirt Jacket

MATERIALS

- Red boy's sweatshirt with set-in sleeves★
- Yellow print or plaid fleece: ½ yard for XS or S; ¾ yard for M; 1 yard for L
- ⅜ yard of red print fleece for binding and scarf
- Assorted felt squares for appliqués
- Eight ½" to 1" assorted colored buttons
- Yellow embroidery floss

★*Note:* Machine quilting causes the fabric to pull in; the extra fabric in a boy's sweatshirt allows for this "shrinkage." For size 4-5, buy XS; size 6-7, buy S; size 8-10, buy M; size 12-14, buy L.

PREPARING THE PIECES

1. With scissors, carefully cut away the ribbing from the sweatshirt bottom. If needed, use a rotary cutter and ruler to even-up the raw edge. Remove the neck ribbing and the sleeves in the same manner. Set the sleeves aside for now.

2. Lay the sweatshirt on a flat surface and measure across the shirt front under the arm area. Divide this measurement in half and mark the center point. Mark a line down the center of the sweatshirt

SUMMER

WINTER

AUTUMN

SPRING

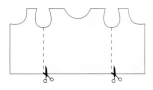

DIAGRAM A

DIAGRAM B

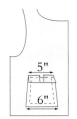

DIAGRAM C

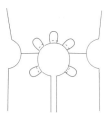

DIAGRAM D

front, from the neck edge to the lower edge. Cut the sweatshirt open along this line, being careful not to cut into the back of the shirt.

3. Remove the shoulder stitching. Referring to Diagram A, open out the sweatshirt on a flat surface and cut the front panels from the back at the underarm "seam."

4. Lay the yellow print fleece face down on the cutting surface and smooth it out. Place each sweatshirt piece (two fronts and a back) right side down on the fleece. Pin the layers together, and cut out the pieces.

5. Leaving the pins in place, machine baste close to the edge of each piece. Remove the pins.

6. Use free-motion quilting to stitch the layers together and create a surface pattern on the jacket. Use the machine's darning foot and drop the feed dogs. Begin at the neckline on each piece. Don't cover the surface too heavily with stitches.

7. Use pinking shears to cut a 6" x 7" piece of fleece for the pocket. Fold over 2" along one short side as shown in Diagram B; pin the flap down. Stitch across the pocket about 1" below the fold to make a casing.

8. Center the pocket on the right front jacket piece, at least 2" from the lower raw edge. Pin the lower edge of the pocket in place, then angle the sides slightly so that the top edge of the pocket is about 1" narrower than the bottom edge; pin. See Diagram C. Begin at the casing stitch line and sew around the pocket ¼" from the pinked edge. The pocket top will be gathered later.

9. Trace and cut the letter and number appliqués from felt using the patterns on pages 28-29. On the left front jacket piece, scatter the numbers and pin in place. Stitch around each with a decorative machine stitch. On the jacket back, scatter the letters and pin in place; stitch. *Note:* Smaller jacket sizes may not need all the letters and numbers.

ASSEMBLY

1. Sew the jacket fronts to the back at the shoulder seams. Clean-finish the seams with a serger or machine zigzag stitch.

2. Cut five neck tabs from jacket scraps using the pattern on page 28. Trim the tab edges with pinking shears. Open the jacket flat;

FREE-MOTION QUILTING

Free-motion machine quilting is a fast and fun way to add surface texture and interest to your projects. To get started, thread the machine with the color of your choice and be certain that the bobbin is full. It's a good idea to have the bobbin thread match the color of the sweatshirt. Change the presser foot to the darning foot, and drop the machine's feed dogs. (If you're not sure how to do this, check your machine's manual for details.) Set the stitch length for 3–4.

Lower the needle into the fabric and begin stitching around in squiggles and loops. You may want to practice on a scrap first to get a rhythm going before you start stitching on your jacket. Avoid stretching and pulling the fleece to move the piece. Instead, use a gentle pressure to guide the stitching where you want it. Avoid overstitching; loose, loopy lines in random patterns are best.

position one neck tab on each side of the front and three tabs evenly spaced on the back. Check that the edges are even with the jacket neck edge. See Diagram D. Pin, then machine baste at the neck edge.

3. Cut two elbow patches from jacket scraps using the pattern on page 28. Trim the edges with pinking shears. Slip each sleeve on the child and mark the elbow with chalk or pins. Take the sleeves off the child and, working from the underarm toward the cuff edge, remove the stitches from approximately 8" of each sleeve seam. Pin the elbow patches in position and stitch around the edges. Hand-stitch over the top of the machine stitches using embroidery floss and a large running stitch.

4. Find the center of the sleeve cap and pin

right sides together to the jacket shoulder seam. Pin the sleeve to the armhole, easing in any fullness. Stitch and clean-finish the seam. Repeat for the second sleeve.

5. Match the underarm seams and side seams; pin. Stitch from the original sleeve seam down the side to the jacket bottom.

6. Lay the jacket out on a flat surface. Trim the front neck area and front bottoms in a gentle curve.

7. Cut a 3" x 60" strip of red print fleece for binding. Beginning at one side seam and working around the jacket in one strip, pin the binding to the right side of the jacket. Stitch the binding using a ¼" seam allowance and overlapping the ends; trim any excess from the end. Fold the binding to the inside of the jacket, and pin. Stitch in the ditch on the front side of the jacket, securing the binding to the inside. Use pinking shears to trim excess binding.

FINISHING

1. Use embroidery floss to sew a colored button to the end of each necktab. Use floss to sew three colored buttons to the flap of the pocket.

2. Use pinking shears to cut a 1" x 12" strip of fleece from jacket scraps. Knot one end

of the strip, leaving a 1" tail, and thread the other end through the pocket casing. Gather the pocket top slightly and tie a knot in the remaining end. Trim the excess with pinking shears.

3. Cut an 8" x 60" strip of red print fleece for the scarf. Clean-finish around the raw edges with a serger or decorative machine stitch. Slip the scarf through the neck-tabs of the jacket.

4. Cut two 3" x 15" pieces of leftover jacket fleece for scarf ties. Trim the edges with pinking shears. Tie one around each end of the scarf. Trim the ends of the ties.

Winter: Fireside Pillow

Finished size 20" x 20"

ASSEMBLY

1. If the blanket is wrinkled, press lightly on the flannel side. Lay the blanket on a flat surface and smooth out. Fold the blanket in half crosswise so that it measures approximately 28" x 48". Cut on the fold line; set one piece aside. You will need only one piece to make the pillow.

2. Pin the cut edges of the flannel and fleece together and machine-baste close to the edges.

3. Fold the piece in half crosswise with the flannel side out. See Diagram E. Pin the cut sides together to within 6" of the top edge. Fold down the top 6" to expose the fleece side, as shown in Diagram F. Set aside.

MATERIALS

■ Purchased 48" x 56" double-sided fleece blanket★

■ ¼ yard each or large scraps of flannel in three contrasting colors

■ 20" x 20" pillow form

■ 1 yard of fusible web

■ Embroidery floss to coordinate with flannel scraps

■ Tapestry or crewel needle

■ Fade-away fabric marker

■ Three size-60 covered button forms

★ *Note:* The blanket shown is flannel on one side and fleece on the other. See Sources for details.

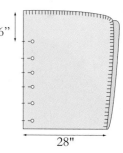

DIAGRAM E

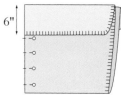

DIAGRAM F

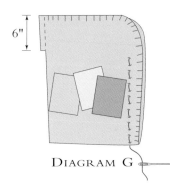

6"

DIAGRAM G

4. From fusible web, cut three rectangles for patches: one 7" x 10", one 8" x 11", and one 9" x 12". Following the manufacturer's instructions, fuse one rectangle to each of the three different flannel scraps. Cut out the rectangles.

5. Referring to the photo, arrange the three flannel rectangles on the flannel pillow square, keeping the rectangles at least 2" from the bottom fold. Pin the rectangles in position, and mark lightly around each one.

6. Remove the pins and unfold the pillow top. Take the top to the ironing board and reposition the flannel rectangles, using the marked lines as a guide to placement. Fuse the rectangles to the pillow top; machine stitch around each one with a decorative stitch. Prairie stitch around the inside edge of each rectangle using embroidery floss.

7. Refold the pillow top with the appliquéd flannel to the inside. Pin the cut edges together. Starting at the bottom fold and using a ¼" seam allowance, sew to within 6" of the top. Make a small clip in the seam allowance above the end of the seam.

8. Turn the pillow flannel side out. Pin the 6" cut edges together. Continue the ¼" seam allowance. See Diagram G.

9. Pin the remaining side of the pillow top and machine stitch along the edge, about ½" inside the blanket's edge stitching. With a double length of contrasting embroidery floss, sew a long running stitch over the top of the line of machine stitches.

10. Fold down the cuff to expose the fleece. Insert the pillow form into the top.

11. Following the manufacturer's instructions, cover three button forms with contrasting flannel scraps. With embroidery floss, sew the buttons to the cuff of the pillow as shown in the photo, sewing the pillow closed at the same time.

MATERIALS

- Purchased jacket pattern
- Blue plaid fleece as required by pattern
- Cotton lining fabric as required by pattern
- Pink, purple, and green felt scraps for appliqués
- 1 yard each of pink and blue ½"-wide double-faced satin ribbon
- 7 crystal or pearl beads or buttons
- Pink and white embroidery floss
- Tapestry or crewel needle for floss
- Pinking shears
- Fade-away fabric marker

ASSEMBLY

1. Cut the jacket pieces from fleece according to the pattern instructions. Cut a second set of jacket pieces from the lining fabric.
2. Trace and cut the tulip and leaf appliqués from felt using the patterns on pages 29–30. Use the pattern to cut the pocket from the jacket fleece; trim the edges using pinking shears.
3. Position the pocket at an angle on the right front jacket, placing it a generous 1¼" in from the center front and lower edges. Pin, and use a fade-away marker to mark the pocket placement. Remove the pocket and set aside.
4. Arrange a large and a small tulip on the jacket front over the pocket opening. The bottoms of the flowers should extend inside the pocket at least ¼". Add a leaf at each side of the tulips. When satisfied with the placement, pin the appliqués in place. Stitch around each flower and leaf with a decorative machine stitch.
5. Reposition the pocket using the marked lines as a guide to placement. Pin, then topstitch around the pocket using a generous ¼" seam allowance. Be sure to leave the pocket top unstitched.
6. Cut a long length of each color of embroidery floss. Hold the colors together and thread the needle, using all 12 strands at once. Sew a decorative ½"-long running stitch around three sides of the pocket, stitching over the top of the machine stitches.
7. Use the same floss to embroider tendrils around the flowers and leaves, referring to Diagram H as a guide to placement.
8. Position the remaining tulip in the center of the left jacket front, approximately 4" to 6" from the hem area. Use the photo and Diagram I as a guide to positioning the flower and leaves. Pin the appliqués in place, then sew them using a machine decorative stitch. Again using 12 strands of floss together, stitch a flower stem and tendrils, referring to the diagram as needed.
9. Assemble the jacket pieces according to the pattern instructions. If the pattern you chose does not include instructions for a lining, simply cut and assemble the lining pieces in the same manner as you did for the jacket. Place the lining and the jacket right sides together and pin generously, matching all seam lines. Begin at the side bottom edge of the jacket and stitch the layers together

DIAGRAM H

DIAGRAM I

using a ½" seam allowance. Be sure to leave at least a 5" to 6" opening to turn the jacket. Clip curves and corners and turn the jacket right side out through the opening.

10. Adjust the sleeve of the jacket and lining, matching the underarm seamlines. Pin the sleeve edges together and stitch with a straight, zigzag, or serger stitch. With matching thread, close the opening in the hem area. Press the jacket from the lining side only.

FINISHING

1. Using embroidery floss, sew a running stitch around the edge of the jacket, approximately ½" from the jacket edge.
2. Stitch the assorted buttons to the ends of the flower tendrils as shown in the photo.
3. Place one ribbon on top of the other, and finger-press to mark the center point. Place the center point in the top center of the pocket and hand-tack in place. Treating them as a single ribbon, tie the ribbons into a bow. Cut off excess streamers at an angle.
4. Turn the sleeves up slightly, then turn them again to form a cuff and expose the lining.

Summer: Fishies and Froggies Beach Set

CUTTING

1. From the purple fleece, cut a 2½" x 54" strip for the tote handle. Trim the remaining piece to 23" x 60" for the tote bag.
2. From the pink fleece, cut an 8" x 16" pocket using pinking shears. Cut two 2½" x 54" strips for the handle.

ASSEMBLY–BLANKET

1. Straighten the edges of the plaid fleece if needed and clean-finish all edges with serger or other machine stitch.
2. Trace and cut three fish from felt using the pattern on page 30. Cut three eyes from scraps. Position an eye on each fish and pin. Stitch around the eye with a decorative machine stitch.
3. Lay the blanket on a flat surface and smooth out. Position the three fish on the blanket in a diagonal line, using the photo as a guide to placement. Pin, and machine stitch around each fish.
4. Cut assorted lengths of jumbo rickrack for the "waves" under each fish. Place one wave under the bottom fish, two waves under the middle fish,

MATERIALS

- 1⅛ yards of plaid fleece for blanket
- ¾ yard of purple fleece for tote bag
- ½ yard of pink fleece for bag handle and pocket
- Four 9" x 12" pieces of green felt for frog legs
- Three 9" x 12" pieces of purple felt for frog bodies
- Assorted 9" x 12" felt pieces for fish appliqués
- Assorted felt and cotton scraps for frog and tote appliqués
- 1 package of jumbo yellow rickrack
- Scraps of rickrack for embellishments
- 8 round shank buttons for eyes
- 8 assorted buttons for embellishments
- Fusible web
- Beans or other filler for frogs
- Craft glue
- Pinking shears
- Fade-away fabric marker
- Black permanent marker

and finally three waves under the top fish. Pin, then sew down the length of the rick-rack to secure.

ASSEMBLY—FROGS

1. The materials listed on page 26 will make four frogs; these instructions are for one frog. Trace and cut frog bodies, legs, and eyes from felt using the patterns on pages 31-32. Use pinking shears to cut out the pieces.

2. Trace the bathing suit patterns on page 31 onto the paper side of fusible web. Following the manufacturer's instructions, fuse the patterns to your chosen bathing suit fabric. Cut out the pieces and fuse to one frog body as shown in the photo. Glue rickrack trim to the bathing suits as shown.

3. For a boy frog, cut a 2" x 4" piece of felt for a bowtie; trim the edges with pinking shears. Pinch the center together, and tie it with thread to secure. Sew a colorful button to the center of the bowtie. Sew the tie to the neck area of the body.

4. For a girl frog, glue a button to the center of the bathing suit top over the rickrack. Tie embroidery floss bows to two buttons, and glue the buttons to the sides of the bathing suit bottom.

5. Pin the frog front to the frog back, wrong sides together. Position the legs, arms, and eyes where indicated on the pattern, inserting them between the body pieces at least ½"; pin. Stitch around the frog body a generous ¼" from the edge, leaving an opening between the legs for stuffing.

6. Sew round shank buttons on the eyes. Fill the frog body with beans or other filler and stitch the opening closed.

ASSEMBLY—TOTE BAG

1. Fold the fleece rectangle in half crosswise, and sew the short edges together using a ¼" seam allowance. Turn the tube right side out.

2. Fold the fabric tube in half crosswise, matching the fold line to the seamline to make a 15" x 23" rectangle. Pin the upper edges together as shown in Diagram J. Set aside.

3. Divide the pocket rectangle crosswise into three sections, and use a fade-away marker to

mark seamlines. Trace and cut glasses, lotion bottle, and key appliqués from felt using the patterns on page 33. Cut a 2" x 2¼" piece of contrasting felt for the bottle label. Use a black marker to write the word "TAN" in block letters. Center the label on the bottle and stitch around the edges to secure.

Place the felt appliqués on the pocket sections in a pleasing manner; pin. Stitch around each with a decorative machine stitch.

4. Position the appliquéd pocket on the folded bag with the bottom of the pocket approximately 3" from the bottom of the bag. Mark placement lines around the pocket fabric. Remove the pocket.

5. Unpin and unfold the bag. Reposition the pocket fabric following the guidelines; pin in place. Topstitch around three sides of the pocket using a ¼" seam allowance; be sure to leave the top edge open. Stitch the compartment seams, reinforcing the seams at the top edge.

6. Refold the bag with right sides together. Pin, making sure the top edges are even. Stitch the sides using a generous ½" seam allowance. Reinforce the stitching at the top edge of the bag.

7. At one lower corner, fold the bag as shown in Diagram K, centering the seam on the folded corner. Measure 1½" in from the corner, and mark a stitching line. Pin, then stitch along the marked line, forming a gusset. Repeat on the opposite corner. Clean-finish the seams with a serger or machine stitch, and turn the bag right side out.

8. Stack the three 54"-long handle strips with the purple strip in the center; pin. Make a mark 8" from one end and stitch across the strips, sewing through all layers. Secure the pinned section to the ironing board and braid the strips to within 8" of the other end. Pin and stitch across as before.

9. Cut the ends of the handle into a fringe if desired. Pin the handle to the sides of the bag and stitch across through all layers. Reinforce the stitching for strength.

10. Cut two 2½" x 17" strips of contrasting fleece from scraps; trim the edges with pinking shears. Tie the strips around the handle where it meets the bag, covering the line of stitches.

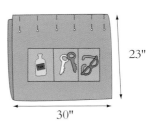

23"

30"

DIAGRAM J

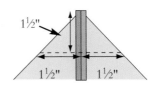

1½"

1½"   1½"

DIAGRAM K

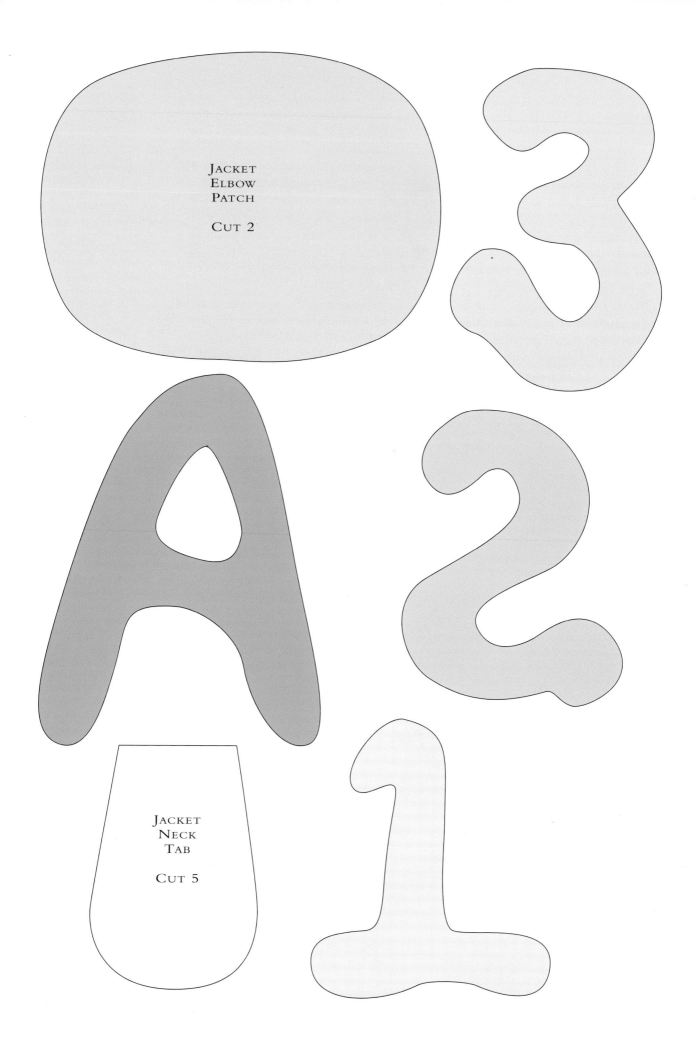

JACKET
ELBOW
PATCH

CUT 2

JACKET
NECK
TAB

CUT 5

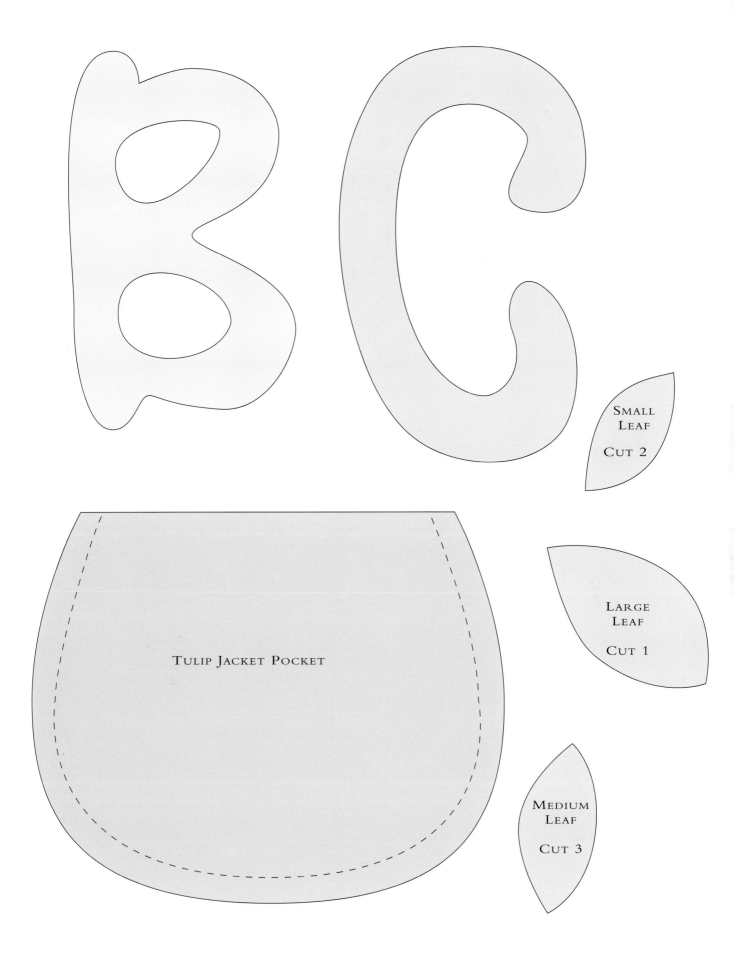

SMALL
LEAF

CUT 2

LARGE
LEAF

CUT 1

TULIP JACKET POCKET

MEDIUM
LEAF

CUT 3

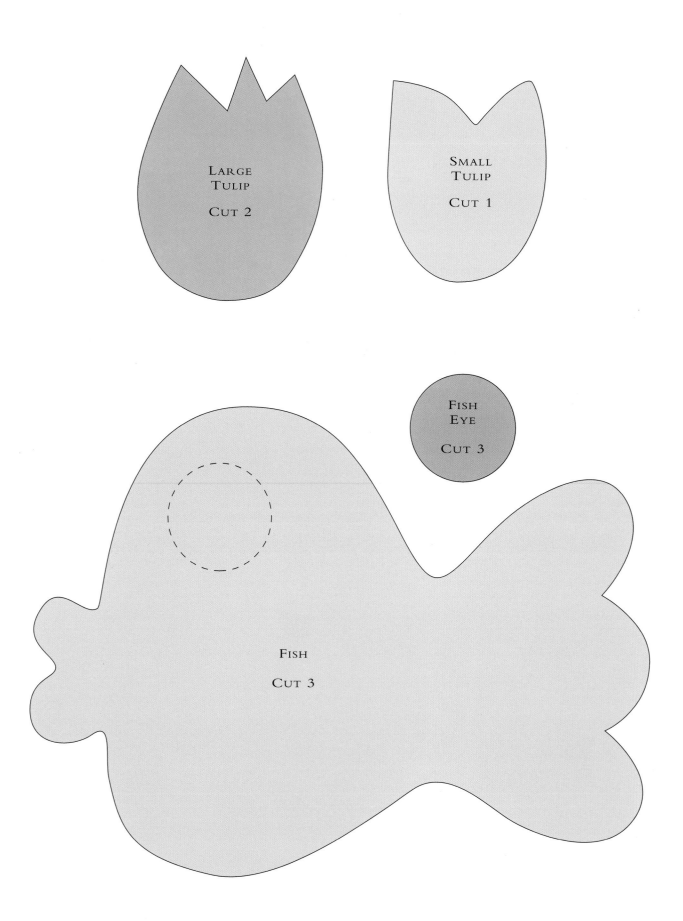

LARGE
TULIP

CUT 2

SMALL
TULIP

CUT 1

FISH
EYE

CUT 3

FISH

CUT 3

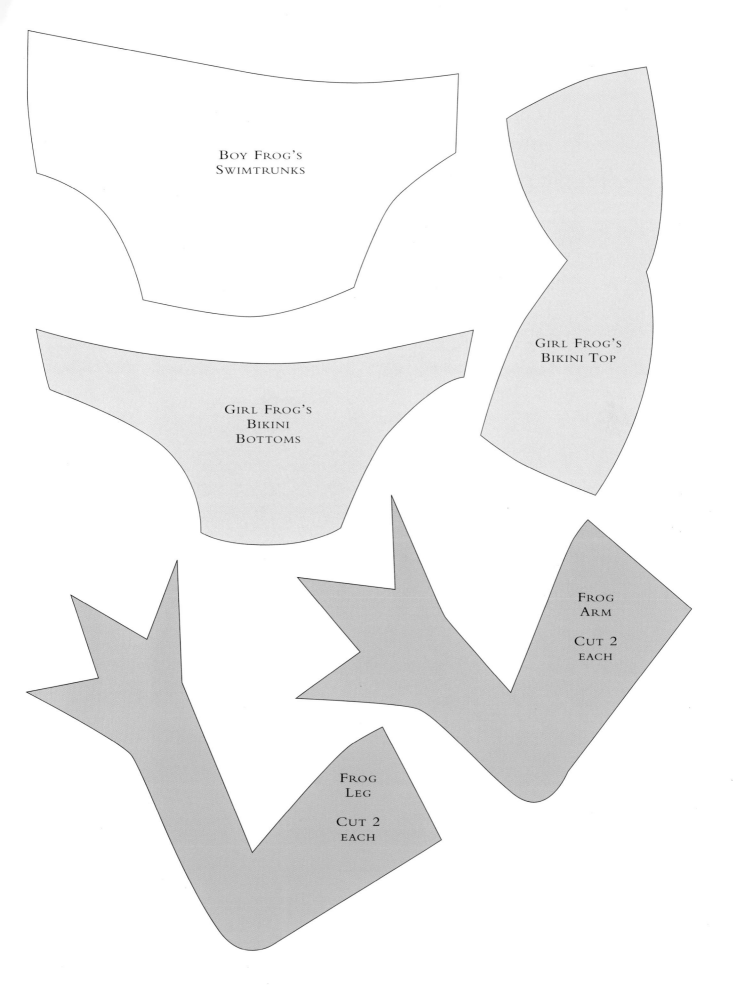

BOY FROG'S
SWIMTRUNKS

GIRL FROG'S
BIKINI TOP

GIRL FROG'S
BIKINI
BOTTOMS

FROG
ARM

CUT 2
EACH

FROG
LEG

CUT 2
EACH

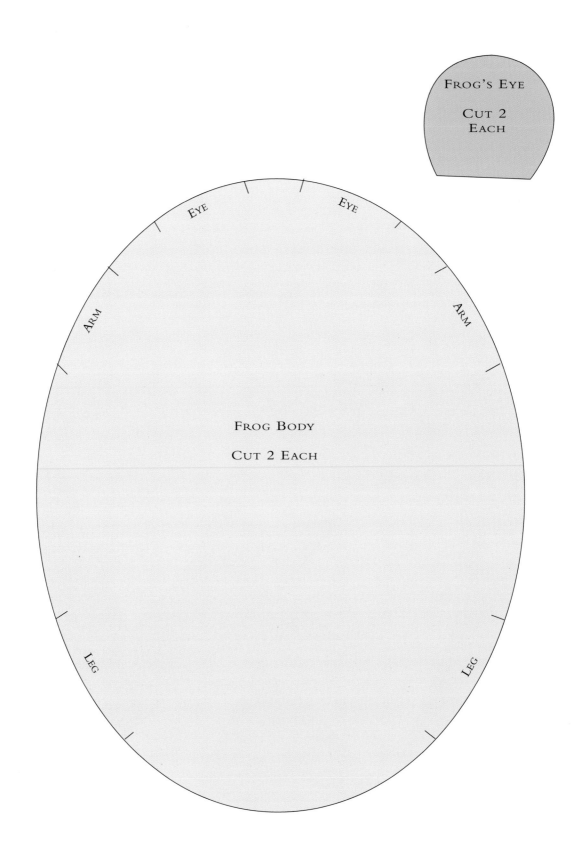

FROG'S EYE

CUT 2
EACH

EYE   EYE

ARM   ARM

FROG BODY

CUT 2 EACH

LEG   LEG

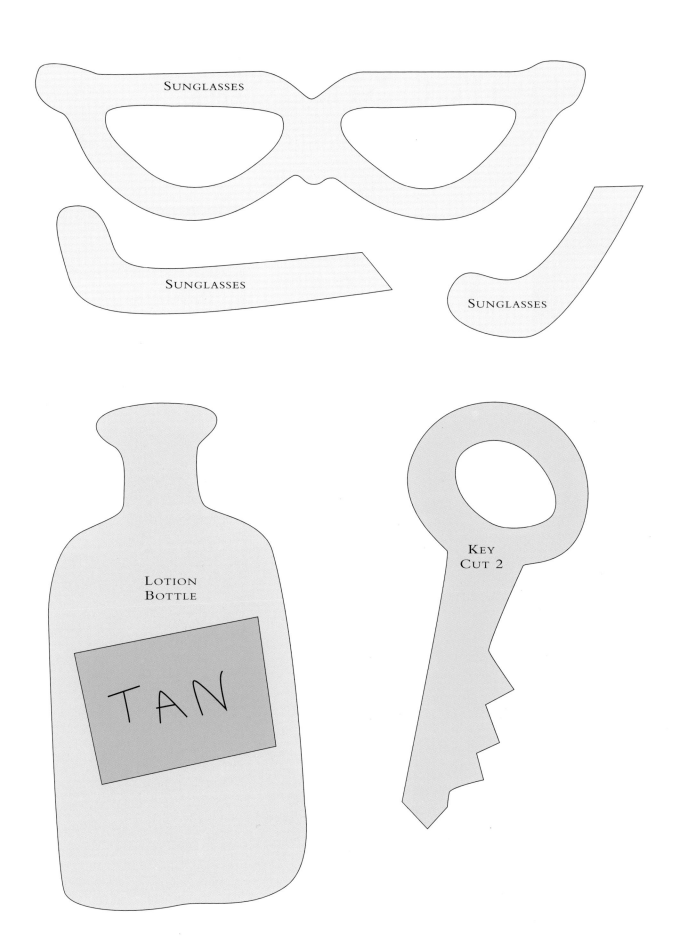

SUNGLASSES

SUNGLASSES

SUNGLASSES

LOTION
BOTTLE

TAN

KEY
CUT 2

Margaret Sindelar

COTTONWOOD CLASSICS

Margaret Sindelar's creative celebration of the seasons begins with a bountiful harvest of Autumn's falling leaves. Four styles of Ultrasuede leaves scattered across a purchased fleece blanket create a cozy throw that folds up into a matching case and becomes a handy pillow.

The approach of winter brings to mind holiday gift-giving, and what child wouldn't love to dress up beanbag toys in these adorable outfits? The festive outfits are easy to make from scraps of fleece and velour.

The lightweight jacket is perfect for spring's sunny days and soft breezes. Margaret cleverly reworked a purchased pattern into a fresh, color-blocked topper accented with beads.

And just for fun, whip up a quick summer beach tote in bright sunny colors with a fleece accent pillow to display your treasured artwork.

Autumn Leaves Throw

Finished pillow size 15" x 23"

MATERIALS

- 50" x 60" tan fleece blanket with finished edge
- ¾ yard of black fleece for pillowcase
- Seven 6" x 8" scraps of cream, blue, lavender, pink, and green Ultrasuede for leaves
- Dark orange #3 pearl cotton
- Fusible web
- Threads to match the Ultrasuede scraps
- Three decorative shank buttons
- Powder blush

ASSEMBLY

1. Using the patterns from pages 40-41, trace a total of seven leaves onto the paper side of the fusible web. Cut loosely around the leaves, then fuse to the wrong side of the Ultrasuede using a press cloth. Cut out the leaves on the traced lines.
2. Arrange six of the leaves across one end of the blanket, reserving a cream leaf for the pillowcase. Pin the leaves in place. *Note:* Do not fuse the leaves to the fleece blanket. The fusible web is used here to add body to the leaves and to make tracing easier. Machine appliqué the leaves to the blanket using a small zigzag stitch and matching threads.

SUMMER

WINTER

AUTUMN

SPRING

3. To make the pillowcase, cut a 24" x 40" rectangle from the black fleece. Referring to Diagram A, fold under a 5" hem along one end, and machine stitch ½" from the folded edge. Position and appliqué the cream leaf 6" from the left side and 1½" up from the hem.

4. Using the pearl cotton, work a buttonhole stitch along the hem.

5. Lay out the rectangle with the appliquéd side face up. Fold the hemmed end up 10" so that the appliquéd leaf is against

the right side of the rectangle. See Diagram B. Fold the other end of the rectangle under 10" as shown in the diagram. Align the side edges, and pin. Stitch the sides with a ½" seam allowance.

6. Turn the pillowcase right side out. Referring to Diagram C, topstitch a 3" flange along both sides. Add decorative buttons to the leaf stem. Add detail to the leaf with powder blush.

7. Fold the blanket and slip it inside the case.

5"

DIAGRAM A

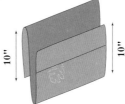

10" **10"**

DIAGRAM B

DIAGRAM C

Winter: Pandy Bear and Candy Bear

Finished size 12" x 20"

MATERIALS

- ¼ yard of green velour for overalls and jumper
- ¼ yard of lightweight red fleece for shirts
- ¼ yard of red-and-white striped cotton for facings, cuffs, collar, and patches
- Scraps of blue Ultrasuede for pockets and straps
- ½ yard of ¼" wide green bias tape
- ¼ yard of ¼" wide elastic
- 8" length of ⅛" wide green rickrack
- Four ⅜" buttons
- Three ⅜" snaps

CUTTING

1. From the green velour, cut two overalls and one back gusset for Pandy Bear using the patterns on page 42–43. Cut one jumper for Candy Bear.

2. From the red fleece, cut two shirts using the pattern. Cut one 2" x 7½" strip for Pandy Bear's collar.

3. From the striped fabric, cut two facings using Candy Bear's jumper pattern. Cut two knee patches as shown on Pandy Bear's overalls pattern. Cut two 2" x 4½" strips for Candy Bear's cuffs and two 1½" x 3" strips for her collar.

4. From blue Ultrasuede, cut two pockets using the pattern, and cut four ⅜" x 5½" strips for the straps. Trim the edges of these strips with pinking shears.

ASSEMBLY
PANDY BEAR'S OUTFIT

1. To make the shirt, align the edges and stitch the sides together using a ¼" seam allowance, starting at the cuff and ending at the lower edge of the shirt. Trim the seam allowances. Referring to the pattern, cut a slit on one side for a back opening.

2. Fold the collar strip in half lengthwise, wrong sides together. Pin the collar to the neck edge, right sides together and raw edges aligned; stitch. Trim the seam allowance, and stand the collar up.

3. Sew a small zigzag stitch along both sides of the back opening to help stabilize the edge. Sew two ⅜" snaps to the collar.

4. To make the overalls, place the pattern pieces right sides together. Starting at the top edge, sew the center front seam, stopping at the dot on the pattern. Sew the center back seam, stopping at the dot on the pattern. Pin the leg/crotch seam and stitch it all at once, starting at the ankle on one leg, sewing up and across the crotch, and continuing down the other leg to the ankle. Clip the seam allowance.

5. With right sides together, match the center of the back gusset to the center back seam; pin. Pin the rest of the gusset to the back of the overalls. Stitch.

6. Trim approximately 1" from the bottom of the striped facing so that it fits inside the overalls. Sew the center back seam on the facing. Place the facing and the overalls right sides together, and pin around the top edge. Slip the ends of the blue Ultrasuede straps between the overalls and the facing, ½" on either side of the center back seam of the facing. Stitch with a ¼" seam allowance, securing toe facing and the straps at the same time. Trim the seam allowance, and turn the facing to the inside of the overalls.

7. Cut a 4" piece of elastic. Pin to the top back edge of the overalls. Stretch the elastic while stitching in place with a narrow zigzag.

8. Center the blue pocket over the front seam and topstitch it in place. Place the shirt and overalls on the bear. Trim the straps to length, and hand-stitch the ends to the inside of the bib, stitching two red buttons to the front of the bib at the same time. Sew a decorative button to the pocket.

CANDY BEAR'S OUTFIT

1. To make the shirt, fold the cuff strips in half lengthwise, wrong sides together, and press. Position the cuffs on the wrong side of the shirt piece, aligning the raw edges, and stitch. Fold the cuffs over to the right side of the shirt. Fold the shirt right sides together, and align the side edges. Stitch the sides together using a ¼" seam allowance, starting at the cuff and ending at the lower edge of the shirt. Trim the seam allowances. The ends of the cuff will be stitched into the seam.

2. Referring to the shirt pattern, cut a slit on one side for a back opening.

3. Turn under ¼" on both short ends of the collar pieces and press. Fold the collar pieces in half lengthwise, wrong sides together, and press. Cut the rickrack in half, and sew one half to each collar piece, stitching it around three sides of the collar. Place the collar pieces face down on the wrong side of the shirt, aligning the raw edges. Stitch the collar in place using a ⅛" seam allowance. Fold the collar over to the right side of the shirt.

4. Sew a small zigzag stitch along both sides of the back opening to help stabilize the edge. Sew a snap at the back neck opening.

5. To make the jumper, sew the center back seam on the jumper and jumper facing. Place the jumper and facing right sides together and pin around the top edge. Slip the ends of the blue Ultrasuede straps between the jumper and the facing, ½" on either side of the center back seam. Finish as for Pandy Bear's overalls.

MATERIALS

- Purchased pattern for a jacket with front facing and back yoke (I used McCall's Pattern #9019)
- Fleece yardage according to pattern requirements: purple for front, back, and sleeves; rose for front facing and collar; burgundy for black yoke
- Four coordinating colors of serger thread for trim
- Four 1¼" buttons
- One package each of large blue, red, green, and clear bugle beads

ASSEMBLY

1. For this jacket, the front facing is sewn on the outside of the front, rather than the inside. Cut out the jacket pieces according to the colors of the fleece. Thread the serger with four different colors of thread.

2. Cut off the seam allowance along the curved edge of the front facings. Cut off the seam allowance along the outside edge of the collar and the bottom edge of the back yoke. Serge-finish these cut edges.

3. Pin the wrong side of the back yoke to the right side of the back. Topstitch along the serged edge. If desired, cut away the upper part of the back (the part under the yoke) to reduce bulk.

4. Pin the front facings to the fronts, and topstitch along the serged edge. If desired, cut away the front under the facing to reduce bulk. Note, however, that the extra layer helps support the buttonholes and buttons.

5. Stitch the shoulder seams and the side seams. Stitch the sleeve seams, and set in the sleeves according to the pattern. Serge-finish the cuff edges of the sleeves.

6. Cut off the seam allowances along the front edges of the jacket; serge-finish these cut edges.

7. Pin and baste the right side of the collar to the wrong side of the jacket. Stitch the collar in place, then serge the edge to secure, trimming the seam allowance. Fold the collar over the serged edge to the outside.

8. Serge around the bottom edge of the jacket. Make buttonholes and sew on the buttons. Randomly hand-stitch bugle beads to the collar. Roll up the sleeves to the desired length.

Summer: Tote Bag

MATERIALS

- Purchased pattern for round tote bag (I used Butterick #3925, View D)
- ½ yard each (or as required by pattern) of green, yellow, and watermelon fleece for sides and lining
- ¼ yard each of hot pink and red fleece for pocket and tote bottom
- Three purchased 3" flower appliqués

ASSEMBLY

1. Cut out the bag pieces and bag lining pieces according to the pattern. Cut a 5" x 6" pocket piece.

2. Place the two outside pieces right sides together and sew, using a ¼" seam allowance. Sew the two lining pieces together.
3. Pin the bag and the lining right sides together, matching the side seams. Starting on one side, stitch together around the top edge of the bag in one continuous seam, stitching up one side of each handle and down the other side. Turn the bag right side out, and topstitch the bag and lining together ¼" in from the top edge.
4. Hem top of pocket ½" along a 6" side. Turn under ¼" on 5" sides. Top stitch to bag positioned over one side seam with bottom edges even.
5. Baste bag and lining together around bottom edge. Place red bag bottom and the lining bottom wrong sides together, baste around outside edge. Pin and stitch bottom to bag sides.
6. Knot handle ends and add flower appliqué.

Summer: Picture Pillow

Finished size 16" x 18"

MATERIALS

- ½ yard of green fleece for border and backing
- 10" x 12" piece of white cotton fabric for picture panel
- ⅛ yard each of yellow, hot pink, and rose fleece for borders
- ⅛ yard of red fleece for piping
- A child's drawing or other artwork
- 10" x 12" piece of lightweight woven interfacing
- 2 yards of ½" piping cord
- 15" x 17" pillow form
- Transfer paper for color laser copies
- Twelve ⅝" decorative shank buttons

CUTTING

1. From the green fleece, cut one 14½" x 16½" back piece and one 4" x 10½" strip.
2. From the yellow fleece, cut one 4" x 10½" strip. From the hot pink and rose fleece, cut one 4" x 14½" strip each.
3. From the red fleece, cut 2¼"-wide strips. Piece together as necessary to make a strip approximately 70" long.

ASSEMBLY

1. Transfer child's artwork centered onto white cotton fabric. Line design with interfacing and trim to 8½" x 10½".
2. Referring to the photo, place the side strips right sides together on the white fabric, and stitch with a ¼" seam allowance. Add the top and bottom strips.
3. Using a zipper foot, cover piping cord with red fleece strip. Pin and stitch piping around outside edge of pillow front.
4. Stitch the pillow front to the back, leaving an opening for turning. Turn right side out; insert pillow form; stitch closed and add buttons.

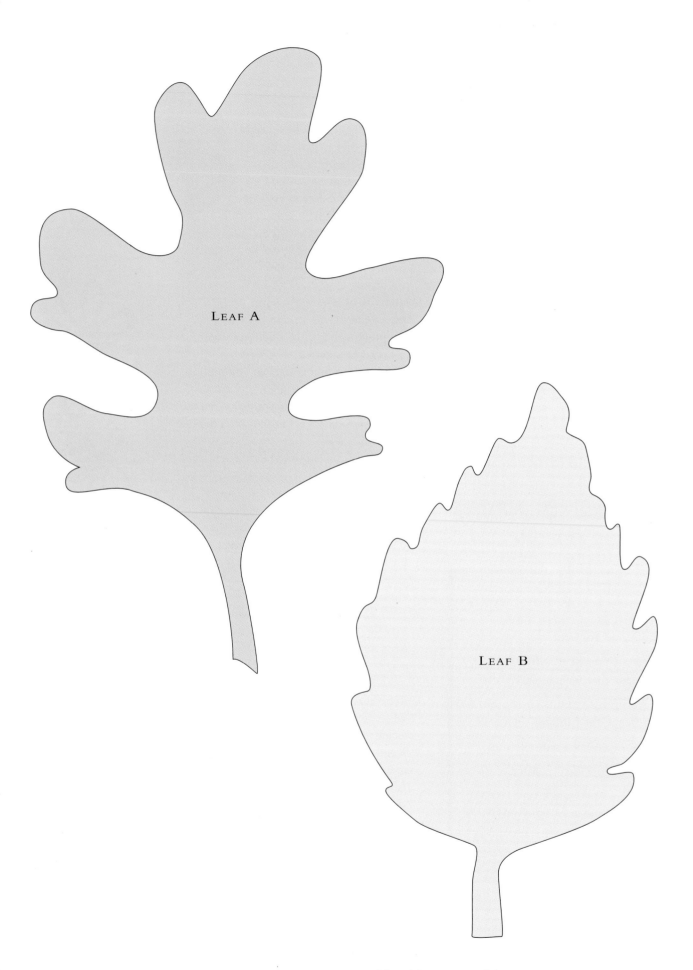

Leaf A

Leaf B

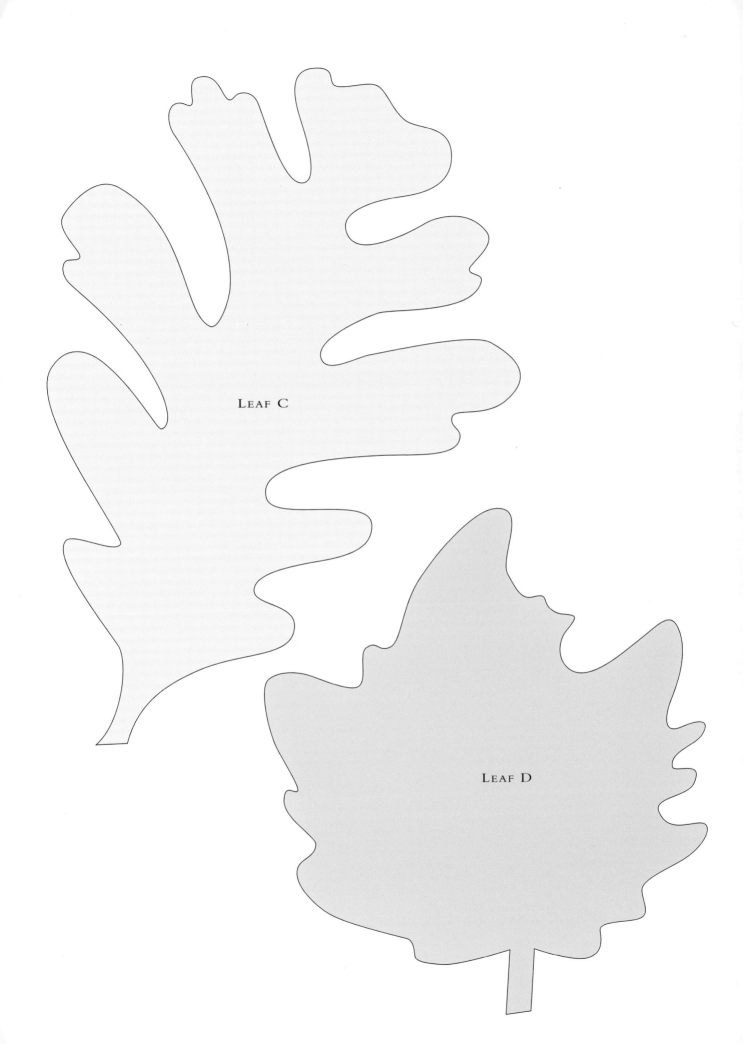

Leaf C

Leaf D

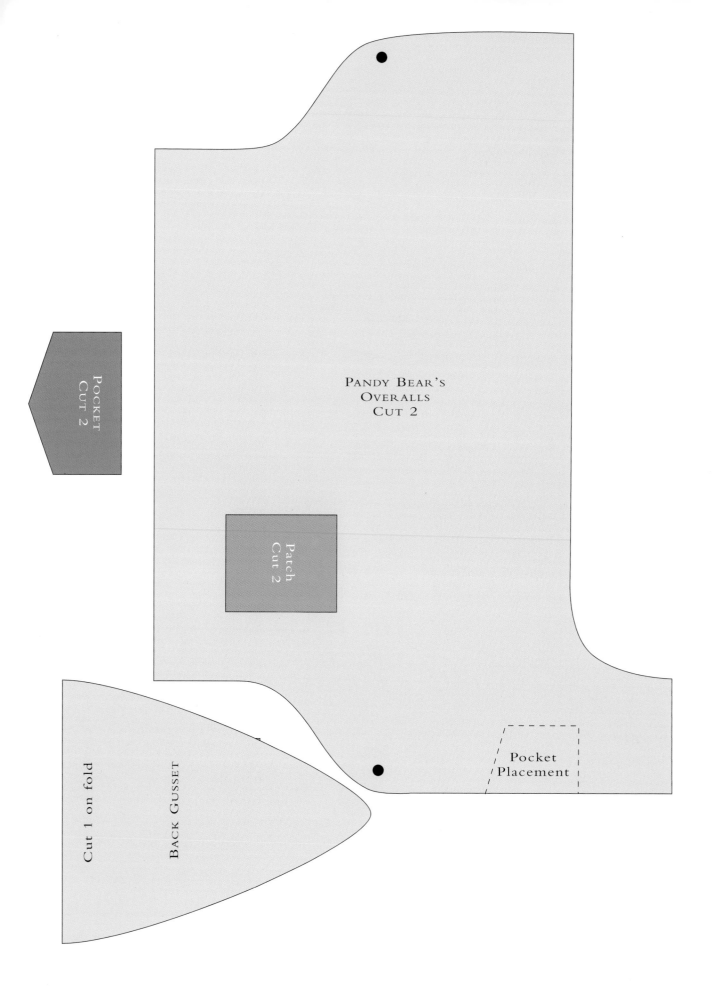

PANDY BEAR'S
OVERALLS
CUT 2

POCKET
CUT 2

Patch
Cut 2

Pocket
Placement

BACK GUSSET

Cut 1 on fold

CANDY BEAR'S
JUMPER

CUT 1 ON FOLD

Trim here for Candy

Fold

Back
opening

Fold

SHIRT
CUT 2 on fold

Trim here for Candy

Janet Carija Brandt

CARIJARTS

Although she had never worked with fleece before, Janet feels that a designer should be able to work with just about any fabric. So, when given the opportunity to create a collection using this versatile material, Janet jumped at the challenge…and loved it! "I really enjoyed working with fleece," Janet says. "In some ways, fleece is a lot like the wool that I often use. It's so easy to work with." Her favorite projects turned out to be the autumn rug because it was so fun and easy, and the dolls because they are so light and cuddly.

Janet's seasonal offerings begin with a great idea for quick-change decorating: a simple-to-make throw rug in warm, rich colors for fall. Janet used a variegated print fleece that almost looks hand-dyed. This rug is so easy, you'll want to make several—maybe one in colors for each season!

To ward off winter's chill in style, whip up the elegant hat, muff, and scarf set—an impressive holiday gift for someone special.

The cheerful babushka dolls arrayed in soft pastel fleece colors are gentle harbingers of spring.

And summer picnics are even more fun when the goodies are carried in a clever trio of nesting buckets crafted from scraps of fleece!

Shades of Autumn Throw Rug

Finished size 22" x 32"

MATERIALS

- 2 yards of 60"-wide double-faced fleece for rug strips
- 1 yard of rug warp or heavy-weight cotton fabric for back

CUTTING

1. From the fleece, cut three 22" x 60" pieces. From two of those pieces, cut twenty-four 2½" x 22" strips each for the rug. From the third piece, cut sixteen 2½" x 22" strips for the rug, plus six 2" x 22" strips for the binding. You should have 64 rug strips.
2. Preshrink the backing fabric by machine washing and drying. Then cut a 22" x 32" rectangle.

ASSEMBLY

1. Referring to Diagram A, use scissors to cut a ½"-wide, 2"-deep fringe along one edge of each of the rug strips.

DIAGRAM A

2. Starting at one short end of the backing fabric, place the uncut edge of a strip along the backing fabric with the fringe

SUMMER

WINTER

AUTUMN

SPRING

DIAGRAM B

hanging off the edge. Machine zigzag in place. See Diagram B.

3. Place the second strip on the backing about ½" above the first strip; zigzag in place. Continue adding strips until the entire backing is covered with fringe.

4. Sew the six binding strips together end to end. Stitch the binding to the front of the rug using a ¼" seam allowance and mitering the corners. Bring the edge to the back side of the rug, and whipstitch the binding to the backing fabric.

• •

Winter: Elegant Ensemble

HAT ASSEMBLY

1. Cut two 7½" x 25½" fleece rectangles for the hat sides. On each rectangle, cut a small notch in the center of one long side. Cut two hat tops using the pattern on page 52.

2. Fold one side piece in half crosswise, right sides together, and sew the short ends together using a ¼" seam allowance. Repeat with the second side piece.

3. With right sides together, match the center notch and seamline of a hat side piece with the notches on a hat top; pin. Pin the top and side together, and stitch using a ¼" seam allowance. Repeat with the second set of side and top pieces; this will form the hat "lining."

MATERIALS

- 1¼ yards of animal-print fleece for hat, muff, and scarf
- ½ yard of lightweight black fleece for muff lining
- 1¼ yard of 2"-wide white fake fur trim for muff (optional)
- 7" zipper for muff lining
- 70 yards of silver metalized polyester/viscose yarn for scarf trim
- 1 yard of ½"-wide flat silver braid for hat trim
- 1 yard each of 1½"-wide silver and silver-and-gold ribbon for hat trim
- 2¼" rhinestone buckle for hat
- About thirty 8mm flatback rhinestones for muff
- Tacky fabric glue

4. Place the hat pieces right sides together, and stitch around the bottom edge, leaving a 3"-long opening for turning. See Diagram C.

5. Turn the hat right side out through the opening; slip-stitch the opening closed.

6. Tuck the lining inside the hat. Turn up the bottom edge of the hat to form a cuff.

7. Cut a length of flat silver braid to fit around the cuff of the hat. Referring to the photo, pin the braid to the hat. Hand-stitch in place, sewing through one layer of fleece only.

8. Place one ribbon on top of the other. Handling them as one, fold the ribbons into soft pleats. Loop the folds through the rhinestone buckle. Position the buckle on the cuff, and hand-stitch in place.

MUFF ASSEMBLY

1. From the print fleece, cut one 15½" x 6½" outside piece, two 3⅜" x 16" bindings, and one 3" x 12" handle. From the black fleece, cut two 13½" x 13¾" lining pieces. Referring to Diagram D for correct dimensions, carefully measure, mark, and recut the two lining pieces as shown.

2. Place the lining pieces right sides together, and sew the 2½" seam on both sides of the pocket section. Unless instructed otherwise, use a ⅜" seam allowance throughout the muff assembly. Baste along the seamline of the pocket.

3. Open out the lining and the pocket. With the lining wrong side up and the pocket right side up, center the zipper face down on the pocket seamline; stitch. See Diagram E. Remove the basting stitches from the pocket seamline.

4. Referring to Diagram F, pin the pocket pieces right sides together and sew around the three sides. Stitch the lining seam on the opposite edge.

5. Fold the muff outside piece in half crosswise, right sides together, and stitch across the short end, forming a tube. Sew two rows of gathering stitches along each open end of the tube; turn to right side.

6. Place the lining inside the muff, wrong sides together. Gather the ends of the muff to fit the lining fabric. See Diagram G. Sew the two layers together at each end.

7. Fold the 3" x 12" handle strip in half lengthwise, right sides together. Using a ¼" seam allowance, sew across one end and down the long side. Turn right side out. Fold the handle in half crosswise, and pin the ends side-by-side at one end of the muff, near the seam.

8. Fold a binding strip in half crosswise, right sides together, and stitch across the short end, forming a loop. Repeat with the second binding strip. Place the binding strips on the muff ends, right sides together and raw edges matching; pin. Sew the bindings in place with a ⅜" seam allowance, stitching the handle ends in place at the same time. Fold the bindings to the inside of the muff, and hand-stitch the edges to the lining.

9. If you wish to add the fur trim, cut two 18½" lengths of the fur. Stitch each into a loop in the same manner as for the binding. Turn under ¼" along one edge, and pin the loop face-up on top of the binding, aligning the folded edge of the fur with the seam line on the binding. Whipstitch the fur to the binding. Bring the opposite edge of the fur to the inside of the muff, and hand-stitch in place.

10. Glue rhinestones to the muff as desired.

SCARF ASSEMBLY

1. Cut a 9" x 60" length of fleece.

2. Cut a length of silver yarn approximately 24" long. Thread a needle with one of the strands, and work a blanket stitch across one short end of the scarf. Don't knot the yarn at either side; instead, leave long (about 7") loose tails at both the beginning and the end. Repeat at the opposite end of the scarf with a second strand of yarn.

3. To make the fringe, begin by cutting two 12" lengths of yarn. Handling the strands as one, fold the yarn in half, and draw the loop through the first blanket stitch about 1".

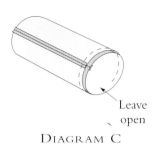

Leave open

DIAGRAM C

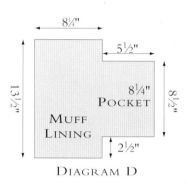

8¼"

5½"

13½"

8¼"
POCKET
8½"

MUFF
LINING

2½"

DIAGRAM D

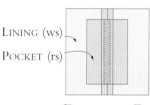

LINING (ws)

POCKET (rs)

DIAGRAM E

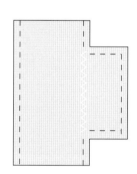

DIAGRAM F

DIAGRAM G

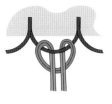

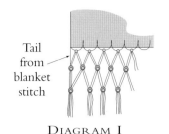

Tail from blanket stitch

DIAGRAM H

DIAGRAM I

Bring the loose ends up through the loop, then gently pull on the ends to tighten the loop against the edge of the scarf. See Diagram H. Repeat in each blanket stitch across both ends of the scarf.

4. Knot the fringe as shown in Diagram I, tying the tails from the blanket stitch into the first and last knots. Trim the ends of the fringe evenly.

Spring: Babushka Dolls

DOLL ASSEMBLY

1. Mix and match the fleece patterns and colors as desired to give the dolls a real folk-art look. For each doll, cut two head/body pieces, four arms, and four legs using the patterns on page 53. Cut a 7½" x 9½" fleece rectangle for the dress sleeve/bodice, and cut a 6" x 23" fleece strip for the skirt. Cut a bib using the pattern on page 54; if desired, taper the ends of the bib as indicated by the dashed lines on the pattern. For the babushka, cut a 5½" square of fleece, then cut it in half diagonally. You will use one triangle for each babushka.

2. Place the two head/body pieces right sides together. Stitch with a ¼" seam allowance, leaving the bottom open for now. To reinforce the seam, sew a second row of stitches around the head, close to the first row on the seam allowance side. Clip at the neck, then trim very close to the double row of stitches. Turn right side out and stuff lightly. Fleece stretches very easily, so be careful not to overstuff and distort the figure.

3. Place the arm pieces right sides together in pairs. Stitch, clip the curves, and turn right side out. Repeat for the legs. Stuff the arms and legs lightly. Hand-stitch the arms to the body with the hands facing upward. Slip the tops of the legs into the bottom of the body with the feet facing forward; stitch across the body, securing all layers.

DIAGRAM J

MATERIALS
(For Two Dolls)

■ Large scraps of at least three different colors of fleece

■ Polyester stuffing

■ Four ⅜" buttons

■ Two ¾" buttons

DRESS ASSEMBLY

1. Fold the sleeve/bodice rectangle into quarters to find the center, and cut a ⅝" quarter circle from the folded point. Open out the rectangle; you should have a 1¼" opening in the center. The opening may seem too small, but it will stretch over the doll's head. If the hole is cut larger, the bodice will not fit nicely around the neck.

2. Fold the rectangle in half lengthwise, right sides together. Referring to Diagram J, machine stitch the underarm seams by sewing in 3" from each side along the bottom edge. Leave the center 3½" unstitched. Turn right side out.

3. Fold the skirt strip in half crosswise, right sides together, and sew across the short end to make a loop. Sew a double row of gathering stitches along one long edge. With right sides together, match the seamline of the skirt to the center back of the bodice. Gather the skirt to fit the bodice; pin, then stitch the pieces together. Turn right side out.

4. Slip the dress over the doll's head. With a needle and doubled thread, sew a row of gathering stitches ¼" from the wrist edge

of each sleeve. Gather the sleeve to fit around the arm. Knot and cut the thread.

5. With a needle and doubled thread, gather and fit the bodice to the doll as indicated in Diagram K, making the dress as long- or short-waisted as you like. Knot and cut the threads.

6. Cut the head opening in the bib. Finish the bib edges with blanket stitches or leave them plain. Slip the bib over the doll's head. Make small gathers or tucks at the waist to fit the bib to the doll: one on each side in the front, and one in the center on the back. Attach the bib to the doll at these points, sewing a ⅜" button at each point on the front and a ¾" button in the center on the back.

7. To make the hair, cut a 2" x 12" strip of fleece. Cut this strip into narrow (about ⅛"-wide) strips. Center the strips on the head and hand-stitch in place. Make one braid on each side of the head. Tie the braid at the bottom with another narrow strip of fleece.

8. Place the triangle babushka on the doll's head and tie the ends together in back, or tuck them under and tack in place. Tack the babushka in several places around the face to secure.

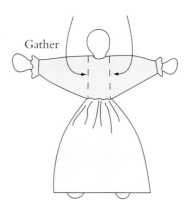

Gather

DIAGRAM K

DIAGRAM L

ASSEMBLY

1. The instructions are written for one bucket. Select a size, and trace the bucket pattern from page 55. Make a template by tracing the pattern four times onto a large sheet of paper as shown in Diagram L. Do not add seam allowances. Cut out the paper template, then use it to trace the pattern onto a piece of stiff interfacing. Do not cut the interfacing at this time. Use the template to trace and cut a lining from the red fleece.

2. Pin randomly cut pieces of fleece to the interfacing pattern, overlapping the pieces about ¼". For example, the stripes on the large bucket were made with long, irregularly cut strips. The pieces on the medium bucket resemble crazy-quilt patches. Use the photo as a guide, but let your fabric selection inspire you. When the pattern is covered with fleece, randomly stitch over the pieces, securing them to the interfacing. Use a zigzag stitch and matching, coordinating, or contrasting thread. Keep the stitching in a mostly vertical pattern to help reinforce the bucket shape and structure.

3. After all the pieces are sewn in place, trim the interfacing along the drawn pattern line. Stay-stitch this new clean edge.

4. Pin the bucket edges right sides together, and stitch using a ⅜" seam allowance. Trim the seam allowance, and turn the bucket right side out.

5. Using the pattern on page 54, trace and cut three bottoms for each bucket: two from the red fleece (one will be the lining), and one from interfacing.

6. Baste the interfacing bottom to the wrong side of one of the red fleece bottoms. With right sides together, pin this bottom to the bucket sides. Sew using a ¼" seam allowance.

MATERIALS
(For Three Buckets)

- ¾ yard of lightweight red fleece for bottoms, linings, and handles
- Assorted fleece scraps for bucket sides
- ¾ yard of heavyweight nonwoven interfacing
- Freezer paper or other large paper

7. Fold the red fleece lining piece in half crosswise, right sides together, and stitch across the short end with a ⅜" seam allowance. Place the lining sides and the remaining bottom piece right sides together; sew around the bottom with a ¼" seam.

8. With right sides together, stitch the bucket and the bucket lining together along the top edge, leaving an opening for turning. Turn right side out, and slip-stitch the opening closed. Tuck the lining into the bucket, and topstitch around the top of the bucket, ¼" from the edge.

9. Cut handles from the red fleece in the following sizes: 2" x 10" for the small bucket, 2" x 13" for the medium bucket, and 2" x 18" for the large bucket. Fold the handle fabric in half lengthwise, right sides together. Sew across one short end and down the long side. Turn the tube right side out. Randomly zigzag stitch along the handle, covering it with stitching to reinforce it. Cut a buttonhole at each end of the handle.

10. Sew a button on each side of the bucket. Button the handles into place.

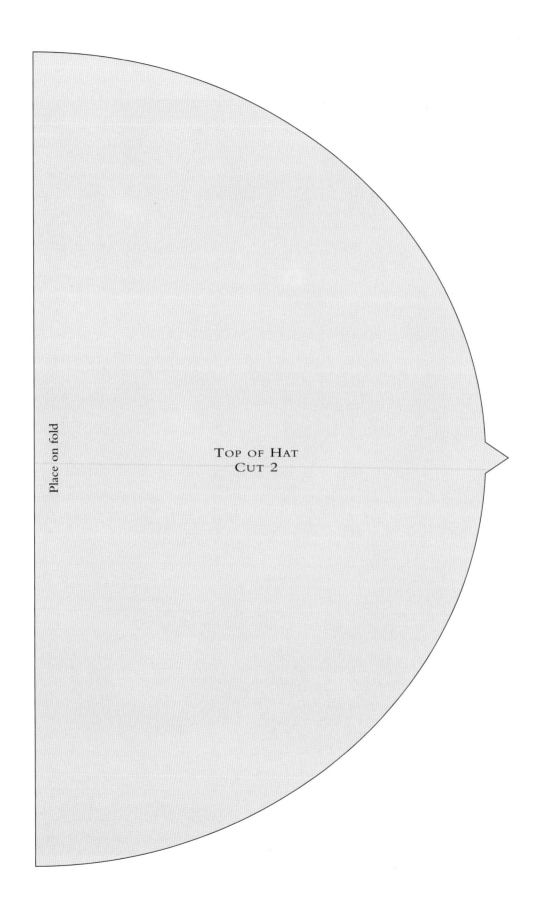

Place on fold

TOP OF HAT
CUT 2

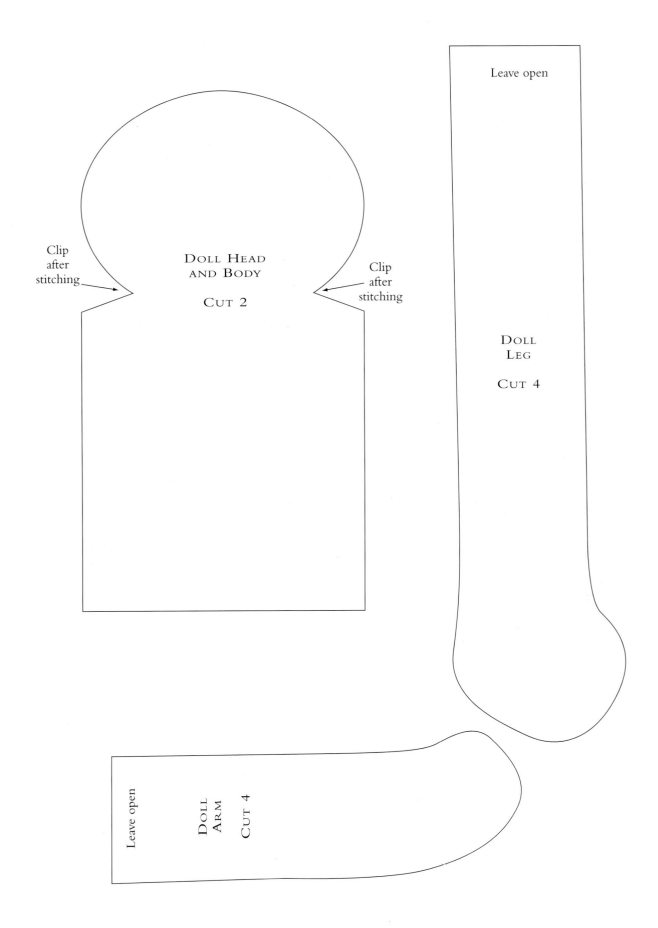

Leave open

DOLL LEG

CUT 4

Clip after stitching

DOLL HEAD AND BODY

CUT 2

Clip after stitching

Leave open

DOLL ARM CUT 4

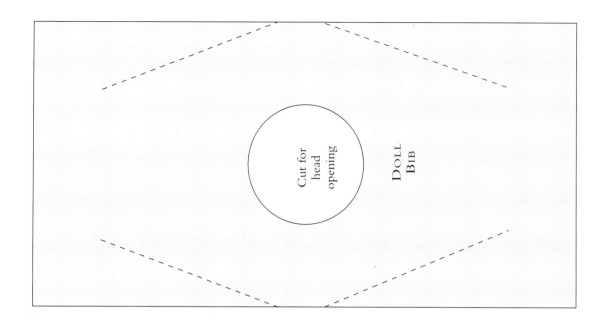

Cut for head opening

DOLL BIB

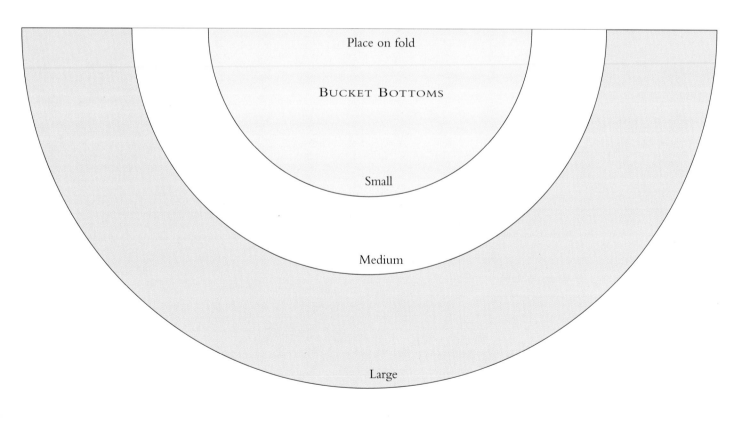

Place on fold

BUCKET BOTTOMS

Small

Medium

Large

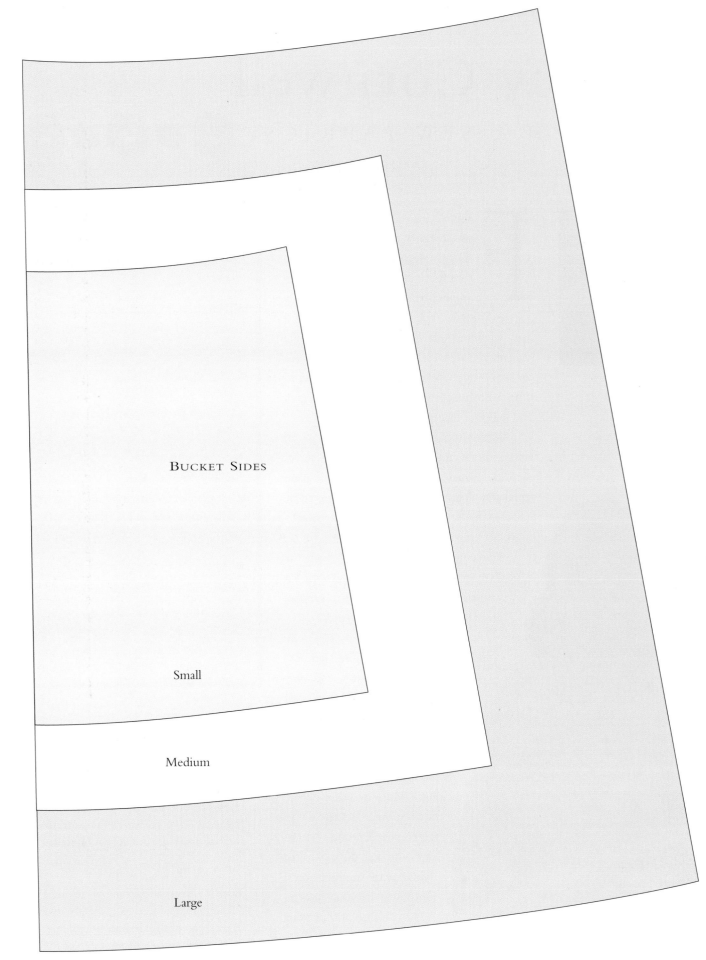

BUCKET SIDES

Small

Medium

Large

Nancy Cornwell

STRETCH & SEW FABRICS®

Fleece is truly a fabric for all seasons, as designer and author Nancy Cornwell proves. Her designs are tastefully classic, yet up-to-the-minute, made of today's latest fleece fabrics. With her help you can turn the most basic of patterns into great wearables or home accent pieces. Her tricks with a double needle or simple appliqué shapes are all you need to turn a ho-hum wardrobe into "Wow! Where did you find that great jacket?"

When the chill of autumn sets in, enjoy an afternoon at the stadium or raking leaves wearing Nancy's Berber pullover with plaid appliqués. This garment has all the rustic charm you'd expect to find in a cozy north-woods lodge.

When the days grow even shorter, the plaid-accented fleece Holiday Bedroom Set is so inviting, you won't want to emerge from your bedroom until spring!

As spring blows into town, toss aside the warmth of that throw and get outside sporting the quick and easy Crossover Vest. It's perfect with anything—jeans, khakis, or even a skirt.

You'll want to make an extra Ribbons and Roses Jacket as a gift for Mom or a friend once they see you decked out in this comfortable and versatile slip-on jacket. We show it in white with summer roses, but try it in your favorite solid color to accent your wardrobe.

Autumn: Berber Pullover

MATERIALS

- Purchased pattern for a plain-front pullover, with or without hood★
- Berber, Sherpa, or Polarfleece® yardage according to pattern
- ⅓ yard of black fusible knit interfacing
- ⅓ yard of small- to medium-size plaid flannel
- ¼ yard each of two small- to medium-size plaid flannels
- Black thread
- Thread to match fleece
- Assorted decorative buttons
- ★ For the pullover shown, I used Stretch & Sew Pattern #375, Hooded Sweatshirt & Tops.

CUTTING

1. Cut the pullover pieces from fleece according to the pattern instructions.
2. From the plaid flannel fabrics, cut one large tree, one medium tree, two small trees, and one bear using the patterns on pages 63-65. Cut two of the patterns on the bias to create additional interest.

ASSEMBLY

1. With right sides together, place each cutout appliqué against a slightly over-sized piece of fusible knit interfacing. Sew around the entire outside edge of the

SUMMER

WINTER

AUTUMN

SPRING

plaid appliqué, using a scant ¼" seam allowance. Trim the excess interfacing. Clip the seam allowance.

2. Cut a slit in the center of the interfacing only, stopping 1" from each end of the appliqué. Clip to the points. Turn the appliqué right side out, turning through the slit.

3. With the plaid side up, press the appliqué, rolling the seam toward the underside and adhering the interfacing.

4. Arrange the appliqués on the pullover front and pin them in place; press to adhere them to the garment. Using the blanket stitch on your sewing machine, stitch the appliqués in place, using the guidelines in the box on page 59.

5. Add additional trees by simply outlining their shapes on the fleece with a machine blanket stitch and black thread, referring to the photo for placement. Arrange and sew on decorative buttons as desired.

6. Finish the pullover according to the pattern instructions.

Winter: Holiday Bedroom Set

CUTTING

1. Measure your bed to determine the length and width of the mattress top, and the drop from the mattress top to the top of the box spring. See Diagram A.

2. Add the drop plus 4" to the mattress length. Add two times the drop plus 4" to the mattress width. This is the size to cut both the mattress pad and the fleece for the throw. It may be necessary to cut two lengths of fleece and join them to achieve the desired width.

3. Again referring to Diagram A, measure the distance from the top of the box spring to the floor. Subtract 3½" from this measurement to determine the width of the plaid portion of the dust ruffle. From the plaid fleece, cut two pieces that are the measured width and 1½ times the mattress length. Cut one piece that is the measured width and 1½ times the mattress width.

4. From the red fleece, cut two strips that are 8" wide and 1½ times the mattress length. Cut one strip that is 8" wide and 1½ times the mattress width.

5. From the muslin, cut a piece that is ½" larger on all sides than the mattress top.

6. From the pillow fleece, cut two 3½" x 17½" pieces and two 3½" x 20" pieces. Cut two 15" x 23½" rectangles.

7. From leftover red and green fleece, cut twenty 3" squares for the pillow.

DIAGRAM A

Mattress length
Mattress width
Drop of floor
Drop of mattress

MATERIALS

- Printed heavyweight fleece for throw
- 3½ yards of plaid fleece for dust ruffle
- 3½ yards of red fleece for trim★
- 1 yard of fleece for pillow back and flange★★
- Quilted mattress pad
- 2 yards of 90"-wide muslin
- Thread to match fleece colors
- 14" x 17" pillow form or polyester stuffing
- 16 buttons for pillow

★ 3½ yards are needed for cutting lengthwise with no piecing. If you don't mind piecing, 1 yard is sufficient.

★★ If you buy 3½ yards for the dust ruffle trim, you will have enough to also make the pillow back and flange.

THROW ASSEMBLY

1. Layer the fleece over the mattress pad, wrong sides together. Serge or machine stitch around all outside edges. Fold under 1" on each edge, then fold again to form a hem. Machine stitch in place.
2. Machine quilt as desired to hold the layers together. The throw shown was quilted with a diagonal grid.

DUST RUFFLE ASSEMBLY

1. Fold each long red strip in half lengthwise, and baste to hold. Pin the raw edges to the right side of the corresponding plaid dust ruffle sections, and stitch using a ½" seam allowance. Serge the seam or finger-press open and topstitch from the right side.
2. Pleat the remaining long raw edge of each plaid dust ruffle section, and pin. When pleating is completed, each section should be the same length as the corresponding side of the muslin piece. Machine baste the pleats in place. See Diagram B.
3. Fold under 1" along the short ends of each dust ruffle section to the wrong side and topstitch or tack in place by hand to hem.
4. Sew each section to the muslin, right sides together. See Diagram C. Serge seams or finger press them toward the muslin and topstitch in place.

PILLOW ASSEMBLY

1. Join the patchwork squares together, two at a time, with both squares right side up and edges butted. See Diagram D. Use a multiple stitch that crosses over the butted seam, such as a triple zigzag, serpentine, honeycomb, or jersey stitch. A simple zigzag is not strong enough to hold the seam together. Set the stitch width so it is at least 5mm wide; 7mm or 9mm is even better.
2. Continue joining squares together in pairs or strips, then join the strips to make a patchwork that is four squares by five squares.

3. With right sides together, sew the 3½" x 17½" fleece strips to the long edges of the patchwork. Finger-press the seams open. Repeat, sewing the 20½"-long strips to the opposite sides of the pillow top. See Diagram E.
4. Fold under 1" along one long edge of each pillow back rectangle. Fold under again and stitch in place to hem. Work four buttonholes on one of the pillow back pieces to coordinate with your selected buttons.
5. Overlap the pillow backs so the piece with the buttonholes is on top and so that the dimensions of the overlapped pieces together are 20½" by 23½". Pin the pieces together.
6. With right sides together, sew the patchwork pillow top to the two-piece pillow back, using a ½" seam allowance. Turn the pillow right side out.
7. Topstitch the pillow in the ditch around the patchwork.
8. Sew buttons in place on the pillow back underneath the buttonholes. Sew buttons on the pillow top at the intersections of the patchwork squares, referring to the photograph for placement.
9. Insert the pillow form or stuff firmly with polyester stuffing and button closed.

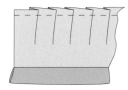

DIAGRAM B

DIAGRAM C

DIAGRAM D

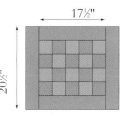

DIAGRAM E

MACHINE BLANKET STITCH GUIDELINES

Begin with a stitch width of 3mm to 3.5mm and a stitch length of 3.5mm to 4mm. Use an edgestitch foot or open-toe appliqué foot for accurate stitch placement. For best results, practice on fabric scraps and adjust the settings according to your personal taste.

Keep the appliqué positioned so the straight stitch is on the garment fabric and the "ladder rung" or bite into the appliqué is at a right angle to it. Where appliqués overlap, stitch the under layer first.

For a bolder blanket stitch, use two strands of black thread or a heavier-weight machine quilting thread.

If your machine doesn't have a blanket stitch, try another variation such as a feather stitch or blind hem stitch.

Waist 5"

Cut away

DIAGRAM F

Front

Waist

5"

DIAGRAM G

PREPARATION

1. On the pattern tracing material, trace one half of the front. Shorten the garment to 5" below the waistline mark. See Diagram F.
2. At the lower edge of the half-front, extend the bottom edge 5" beyond the center front as shown in Diagram G. This creates the overlap.
3. Referring to Diagram G, draw the new center front edge from the extension to the neck/shoulder point. Use this new pattern to cut a right and left front from fleece. Cut one back using the piece from the purchased pattern. Shorten to 5" below the waistline mark.
4. To cut the lower band, add ½" to the upper hip measurement. Cut a strip of fleece 8" wide by this measurement, with the greater stretch going in the length.

ASSEMBLY

1. Sew the fronts to the back at the shoulder seams. Finger-press the seams toward the back and topstitch to secure.
2. Sewing from the wrong side of the fabric, turn under and stitch a ½" hem along the center front and back neck edges. For best results, align the left toe of the presser foot with the raw edge of the hem, and move the needle position to the far left. The bobbin thread will sink into the loft of the fleece, making those stitches virtually invisible. Stitching from the wrong side in this manner is easier and offers a better

MATERIALS

- Purchased pattern for loose-fitting, plain-front sweatshirt with dropped shoulders★
- 1 yard of light to midweight fleece with at least 25% stretch★★
- Thread to match
- Pattern tracing material
- Optional embellishments:
  - Metallic thread
  - Cotton fabric scraps for yo-yos
  - Ultrasuede scraps for leaves
  - 12 assorted ceramic or jewel buttons

★ For the vest shown, I used Stretch & Sew Pattern #303, Sweatshirts.

★★To determine if fabric has enough stretch, pinch 10" on crossgrain and stretch. It should stretch comfortably to 12½".

opportunity for even stitching. It allows you to see exactly how much you're turning under and eliminates the possibility of missing the edge. If desired, using metallic thread and a zigzag stitch, topstitch the center front and back neck edges from the right side.

3. Sew the fronts to the back at the side seams.
4. Turn under a ½" hem at the armholes and stitch from the wrong side as in Step 2.
5. Lap the right front over the left front, overlapping 9". See Diagram H. Sew two rows of gathering stitches along the lower edges of the vest.
6. With right sides together, sew the lower band into a loop, stitching the short ends together with a ¼" seam allowance.
7. Fold the band in half, wrong sides together. Divide the band into quarters and mark with pins. Divide the lower edge of the vest into quarters and mark with pins.

8. Matching quarter marks, pin the lower band to the right side of the vest, placing the lower band seam at the center back. Draw up the gathering stitches until the vest is slightly larger than the band.

9. With the band on top and the vest against the machine, stretch the band to fit the vest as you sew. Remove the gathering stitches.

10. To embellish the vest, make seven yo-yos from assorted cotton fabrics, using a variety of sizes of circle templates, as desired. With a hand-sewing needle and a double strand of thread, fold under the edge of the circle and stitch in place with a running stitch. Pull the thread to gather; knot thread.

11. Create and cut three leaf shapes from Ultrasuede scraps using a pinking shears.

12. Attach the yo-yos to the vest by hand-sewing a button to them through the center of the yo-yo and onto the vest. For yo-yos with leaves underneath, pinch the center of the leaf to pleat it. Stitch all pieces to the vest at once: button, yo-yo, and leaves. Sew other buttons directly to the vest, referring to the photograph for placement.

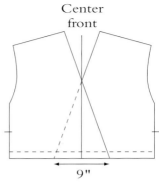

Center front

9"

DIAGRAM H

Summer: Ribbons and Roses Jacket

PREPARATION

1. Trace the front pattern piece onto pattern tracing material. Measure from the shoulder seamline to the hemline, as shown in Diagram I, and divide this measurement into thirds. Draw horizontal lines across the front pattern to divide it into thirds, as shown in Diagram J.

2. Using the bias lines on your cutting mat or clear ruler, draw a 45° line on the upper front section, drawing from the center front up to the shoulder armhole edge, as shown in Diagram K.

3. Fold the upper front section onto the middle front section and trace the 45° line onto the middle section, as shown in Diagram L.

4. Fold the middle section over onto the lower front section, and again trace the 45° line to create a chevron effect. See Diagram M. *Note:* Depending upon the garment size and length, your diagonal lines may not look exactly as they do here. They do not need to reach from horizontal seam line to horizontal seam line. They merely serve as a guideline for pintuck placement.

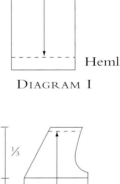

Shoulder seam

Hemline

DIAGRAM I

⅓

⅓

⅓

DIAGRAM J

MATERIALS

- Purchased pattern for cardigan-style jacket★

- Solid color midweight fleece, yardage according to pattern plus ½ yard

- 2 large spools of thread to match fleece

- Pattern tracing material

- 4.0/80 double needle

- 3-groove pintuck foot

- Optional Embellishments:

  - 8 yards of 1"-wide ribbon

  - 38 satin ribbon roses

  - 34 small embroidered floral appliqués

★ For the jacket shown I used Stretch & Sew Pattern #1083, Cardigans.

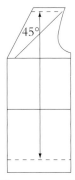

DIAGRAM K

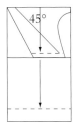

DIAGRAM L

DIAGRAM M

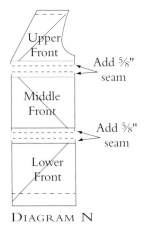

Upper Front

Add ⅝" seam

Middle Front

Add ⅝" seam

Lower Front

DIAGRAM N

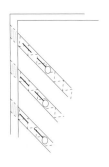

DIAGRAM O

5. Cut the front pattern piece apart on the drawn horizontal lines. Then, using another piece of pattern tracing material, trace separate upper, middle, and lower front sections, adding ⅝" seam allowance to all newly cut edges. Draw in straight-of-grain lines and 45° lines. Label new pattern pieces with all pertinent information. See Diagram N.

6. Cut out back and sleeves, plus any facings, pockets, or hem bands in your chosen pattern.

7. Create pin-tucked fabric following the directions in the box below. Then cut two upper fronts, two middle fronts, and two lower fronts as follows: Cut each front section on the bias, using each 45° line as an alignment line. Center the angled line directly on top of a pintuck. Cut each front section on a single layer of fabric, fabric right side up. Remember to flip pattern pieces over for right and left sides of garment.

ASSEMBLY

1. With right sides together, pin the upper front to the middle front, matching pintucks exactly. To maintain alignment, insert a pin into the center of the top pintuck and exit the pin exactly through the center of the bottom pintuck. Pin-match every pintuck. See Diagram O.

2. Using a ⅜" seam allowance, baste the upper front to the middle front, carefully sewing over the pins. Check the seam to see that pintucks match exactly. Correct if necessary, then stitch the seam. Finger-press the seam open.

3. Repeat Steps 2 and 3 to attach the middle front to the lower front. Repeat for the other jacket front.

4. Stitching from the right side of the garment, topstitch ¼" on each side of all horizontal front seams.

5. Finish the garment according to the pattern directions.

6. To add ribbon and roses embellishments, hand tack the ribbon in place in the channels between the pintucking. The ribbon is knotted every 3½". Begin at the shoulder and tack the end in place, and continue tacking at the midpoint between each knot. Continue following the angle of the pintucking, turning 90° at the middle front section, and again at the lower front section. Add additional rows of ribbon every five rows of pintucking, referring to the photograph. Add satin ribbons by hand over the top of the ribbon, centered between the knots. Add the embroidered floral appliqués in the rows midway between the ribboned rows, again referring to the photograph for placement.

HERE ARE SOME TIPS FOR TROUBLE-FREE PINTUCKING: Insert the double needle and thread the machine with two spools of matching thread. If your machine doesn't have two separate spool pins, wind thread on a bobbin and put the bobbin on the spool pin first, followed by the spool of thread. Make sure the spools are winding off in different directions to avoid tangling.

Keep the threads separate—with one on one side of the tension disk and the other on the opposite side. If your machine has two thread guides before the needle, use one thread in each guide.

Experiment on a scrap. Stitch on the lengthwise grain with the 3-groove pintuck foot, and tighten the upper tension until you achieve a raised welt.

Stitch pintuck rows ¾" apart, parallel to the selvage. Use a quilt bar, seam guide, or edge guide as a spacer bar for accurately spaced rows.

Small Tree

Medium Tree

BEAR TEMPLATE

LARGE TREE

BOTTOM

LARGE TREE

TOP

Judith Carter & Leigh Anne Roach

CUSTOM THREADS

Halloween is a holiday that lets adults be kids again. Judith and Leigh Anne had fun making their goblin's version of the classic checkers and checkerboard. An orange and black pieced checkerboard plus jack-o'-lantern and black cat checkers may tempt even the Great Pumpkin to pull up a chair for an old-fashioned game of checkers. And for kids on the go, the drawstrings on the checkerboard transform it into an easy storage pouch.

To brighten up spirits in a hurry, this talented design duo created a bright, cheery red pillow with a fleece latch-hooked heart to chase away the winter blahs.

With spring rains bringing spring flowers, a fleece pillow in orange, yellow, and pink adds a splash of welcome color to bloom indoors.

For summer, kids can sleep over with friends, or camp out in the backyard. This moon and stars sleeping bag will be a hit with the 10-and-under crowd!

Autumn: Halloween Checkers Set

Finished size 31" square

MATERIALS

- 1 yard of black fleece for patchwork, borders, and cat checkers
- ½ yard of orange fleece for patchwork and jack-o-lantern checkers
- Scraps of green and yellow fleece for checkers
- 4 yards of black cording
- 4 yards of orange cording
- 4 yards of ⅝"-wide black grosgrain ribbon
- Fusible web
- Orange embroidery floss
- 12 orange and 12 black pony beads
- Two 8 oz. bags of poly pellets
- 24 black ⅜" buttons

CUTTING

1. From the black fleece, cut two 4" x 40" strips, two 4" x 28" strips, and four 3½" x 30" strips. Cut twenty-four 3½"-diameter circles; trim the edges with pinking shears. Cut twelve 1¼" squares; cut in half diagonally.
2. From the orange fleece, cut four 3½" x 30" strips. Cut twenty-four 3½"-diameter circles and trim with pinking shears.
3. From the green fleece, cut twelve ½" x 2" pieces for jack-o'-lantern stems.

SUMMER

WINTER

AUTUMN

SPRING

CHECKERBOARD

1. Assemble the black and orange 3½" x 30" strips to form a strip set as shown in Diagram A. Flatlock the seams on a serger if desired, or zigzag. Use a rotary cutter, ruler, and mat to cut the strip set into eight 3½" strips. Referring to the diagram, arrange the strips in a checkerboard pattern; stitch.

2. Referring to Diagram B, stitch the black 4" x 28" strips to the top and bottom of the checkerboard; trim even with the sides. Stitch the remaining black strips to the sides of the checkerboard; trim even with the top and bottom.

3. For the drawstring pouch shown on page 66, place 2 yards of black cording and 2 yards of orange cording together; thread 6 black and 6 orange pony beads alternately on the cording. Center the beads in the middle of the cording and tie a knot on both ends to hold the beads in place. Repeat with the remaining cording and beads. Fold over approximately ½" on the ends and stitch securely to the back side of the border at the corners, as shown in Diagram C.

4. Referring to the diagram, cut four pieces of grosgrain ribbon and position them over the cording. Place the ribbon on the border, just outside the edge of the checkerboard. Turn under the ends; pin and baste each long edge, having the cording sandwiched between the ribbon and border. Stitch, using a zipper foot if necessary to avoid stitching through the cording.

CHECKERS

1. On the paper side of the fusible web, trace 24 cat eyes, 24 jack-o'-lantern eyes, and 12 jack-o'-lantern mouths. Following the manufacturer's instructions, apply the fusible web to one side of the yellow fleece. Cut out the eyes and mouths. Fuse the cat eyes to 12 black circles and fuse jack-o'-lantern eyes and mouths to 12 orange circles.

2. For the cat nose, attach the black button with a double length of embroidery floss. Tie the floss and cut, leaving 1¾"-long ends for whiskers.

3. For the cat ears, fold a black triangle so the acute angles meet and the right angle forms the point of the ear. Pin the folded ear to the cat face circle, having the folded edge ¼" inside the cut edge of the circle so that the ear will be caught in the seam. Repeat for all ears. Fold the green strips in half and pin to the top of the jack-o'-lanterns, having the edges of the strips ¼" inside the cut edges of the circle.

4. Pin the remaining black circles to the back side of the cat faces and the remaining orange circles to the back side of the jack-o'-lanterns; stitch scant ¼" seams, leaving approximately 2" open for stuffing. Pour poly pellets in the checkers to desired fullness; stitch closed. For best results, place a scrap of fabric or interfacing over the pellets in the checker to help keep pellets contained and away from the machine needle.

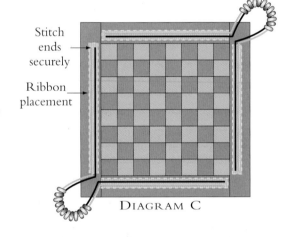

DIAGRAM A

DIAGRAM B

Stitch ends securely

Ribbon placement

DIAGRAM C

Winter: Valentine Heart Pillow

Finished size 15" x 22"

MATERIALS

- 1 yard of red fleece for the pillow cover and heart
- ¼ yard each of magenta, pink print, and white fleece for the heart
- 12" square of 4-squares-to-the-inch Zweigart canvas
- 12" square of fusible adhesive
- 2 yards of 1"-wide fusible web
- Red thread to match fleece
- 15" square pillow form
- Ten ⅝" white heart-shaped buttons
- Size G/6 crochet hook
- Fine point permanent marker
- Masking tape

CUTTING

1. From the red fleece, cut one 31" x 35" piece for the pillow. Cut one 3" x 28" strip for the heart.
2. From the pink print and the white fleece, cut two 3" x 35" strips each for the heart. From the Magenta fleece, cut one 3" x 40" strip.

ASSEMBLY

1. Tape the sides of the canvas using masking tape. Center and trace the heart pattern from page 72 onto the canvas using the marker.
2. Cut the 3"-wide fleece strips into ¼" pieces, cutting along the lengthwise grain as shown in Diagram D.

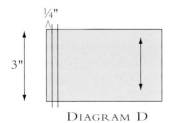

DIAGRAM D

3. Beginning at the outer edge and continuing until the center is filled, use the crochet hook to latch-hook the heart, using one strip per hole in the canvas. See Diagram E.
4. Trim the canvas 1" from the design edge. Turn back the canvas edge and lightly press on the wrong side of the heart using a warm iron. Following the manufacturer's instructions, cut and adhere the adhesive to the back of the heart.
5. Fold the red fleece in half, wrong sides together. Center and pin the heart to one side of the fleece. Unfold the fleece, and adhere the heart using an iron and pressing with the heart face down on a lightly padded surface.
6. Fold the fleece in half, right sides together, and sew a ½" seam along the 31" edge, creating a tube. Turn the sides under 4" and hem each end of the tube. Use the 1"-wide fusible web and follow the manufacturer's instructions.
7. Turn the tube right side out, and insert the pillow form. Sew the pillow closed at each end with the buttons and red thread.

DIAGRAM E

Spring: Flower Pillow

18" diameter

MATERIALS

- ⅓ yard each of yellow, orange, and pink fleece
- 6" x 10" piece of green fleece
- ⅓ yard of nonwoven interfacing or muslin
- ⅓ yard of iron-on interfacing for knits
- 2½" x 2½" scrap of nylon tulle
- Orange embroidery floss
- Three 8 oz. bags of poly pellets
- Buttons for bug: 1¼" green, ⅞" pink, ½" blue
- Cutting mat and rotary cutter with plain or decorative blades (optional)

CUTTING

1. From the yellow fleece, cut one 12" square and one 10½" circle. Cut four petals using the pattern on page 73.
2. From the orange fleece, cut one 12" square and three petals.
3. From the pink fleece, cut four petals. From the green fleece, cut 1 leaf using the pattern on page 74.
4. From the nonwoven interfacing, cut two 9¾" circles.

ASSEMBLY

1. Place the two interfacing circles together and stitch with a ¼" seam allowance, leaving a 3" opening to insert pellets. Clip the seams and turn. Pour three bags of pellets into the pillow; whipstitch the opening closed.
2. Cut the yellow and orange squares into 1" strips, but stop cutting 1" from one end of each square so that the strips remain attached at one end. If desired, use a decorative blade on your rotary cutter. Place the cut strips perpendicular to each other and weave the strips together.
3. Cut a piece of iron-on interfacing slightly larger than the woven strips. Apply the interfacing to one side of the strips, following the manufacturer's instructions. Mark a 10½"-diameter circle on the fused, woven strips; stitch ¼" in from the marked line. Cut on the marked line.
4. For the petals and leaf, bring the dots together to form a pleat; pin. Arrange the petals and leaves around the woven center, placing the pleated edge even with the edge of the woven center. Pin and stitch, using a ¼" seam allowance.
5. Place the yellow circle over the center with the petals and leaf sandwiched inside. Pin and stitch ¾" from the edge, leaving an 8" opening for turning. Cut notches in the seam allowance; turn right side out. Insert the poly pellet pillow form. Pin the opening closed along the seamline; sew with a blind stitch.
6. Accordian-pleat the nylon tulle scrap. Insert the tulle between the large and medium buttons to make the bug's wings. Sew the buttons and wings to the flower center using a length of orange embroidery floss. Sew the small button to the pillow to make a head for the bug, using orange floss and sewing from the front of the button. Leave a thread tail, insert the needle through the pillow and bring it back out to the front of the button. Tie the floss tails together, trim to approximately 2", and tie a knot in the end of the thread to make antennae.

Approximately 30" x 66"

MATERIALS

- 2 yards of navy fleece for bag
- ⅝ yard of white fleece for moon
- ⅓ yard of light blue fleece for clouds
- ⅓ yard of silver lamé fabric for piping
- Scraps of gold and red fleece for appliqués
- 1¾ yards of ¼" cord
- 1 yard of fusible web
- 36" navy zipper
- Small amount of polyester fiberfill
- White, light blue, and navy thread to match fleece
- Five ¾" star buttons and two ⅞" buttons for stars and eyes (optional)
- Red, gold, and blue #5 pearl cotton

CUTTING

1. Fold the navy fleece in half lengthwise. Measure 21" from one end, and cut across the fabric, cutting through both layers. See Diagram F.

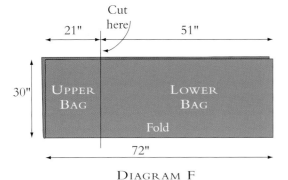

DIAGRAM F

2. Referring to Diagram G, cut both layers of the top in a gentle curve. Cut the pieces apart on the fold. From the scraps, cut one eye and one reverse eye using the pattern on page 75.

3. Draw an 18½" circle onto the paper side of a piece of fusible web; cut just outside the drawn line. Fuse to the white fleece, and cut on the drawn line.

4. Trace the cloud pattern pieces on page 76–77 and enlarge 150 percent. From the light blue fleece, cut one cloud and one reverse cloud.

5. Trace the patterns from page 75 onto the paper side of the fusible web. You will need one eyebrow, one reverse eyebrow, one eye, one reverse eye, one nose, one large star, two medium stars, two small stars, and one mouth. Following the manufacturer's instructions, apply the eyebrows, nose, and stars to one side of the gold fleece. Apply the mouth to the red fleece, and the eyes to the blue fleece. Cut out along the drawn lines.

6. From the silver lamé, cut enough 1½"-wide bias strips to cover the cord. Sew the strips end-to-end using diagonal seams.

ASSEMBLY

1. Referring to the photo for placement, fuse the facial features to the moon.

2. Cover the cord with the silver lamé strip, using a zipper foot and a ½" seam allowance. Trim the seam allowance to ¼", and sew the silver piping around the moon. Fuse the moon and stars to the front upper bag. Add buttons, if desired, and blanket-stitch around the facial features with the pearl cotton.

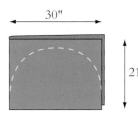

DIAGRAM G

3. With right sides together, sew the front clouds to the back upper bag along the side seam. Sew the back clouds to the front upper bag along the side seam. Place the two sections right sides together, and sew around the top edge of the upper bag and clouds, as shown in Diagram H. Press lightly with a warm iron and turn right side out.

4. Fold the lower bag in half lengthwise and sew the zipper in the side seam. Sew the remaining section of the side seam and the bottom edge.

5. Stuff the clouds with a small amount of fiberfill; pin the bottom edge closed. Pin the clouds and upper bag to the lower bag, having raw edges even. Make sure that the moon will be in the correct position after stitching. Sew all three layers together using a ½" seam allowance. Zigzag the seam edges together. Lightly press the seam toward the lower bag and stitch the seam to the lower bag.

DIAGRAM H

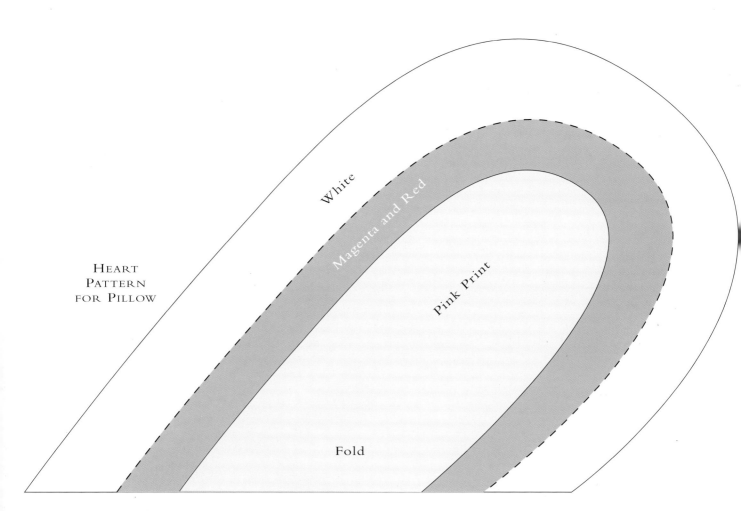

HEART PATTERN FOR PILLOW

White

Magenta and Red

Pink Print

Fold

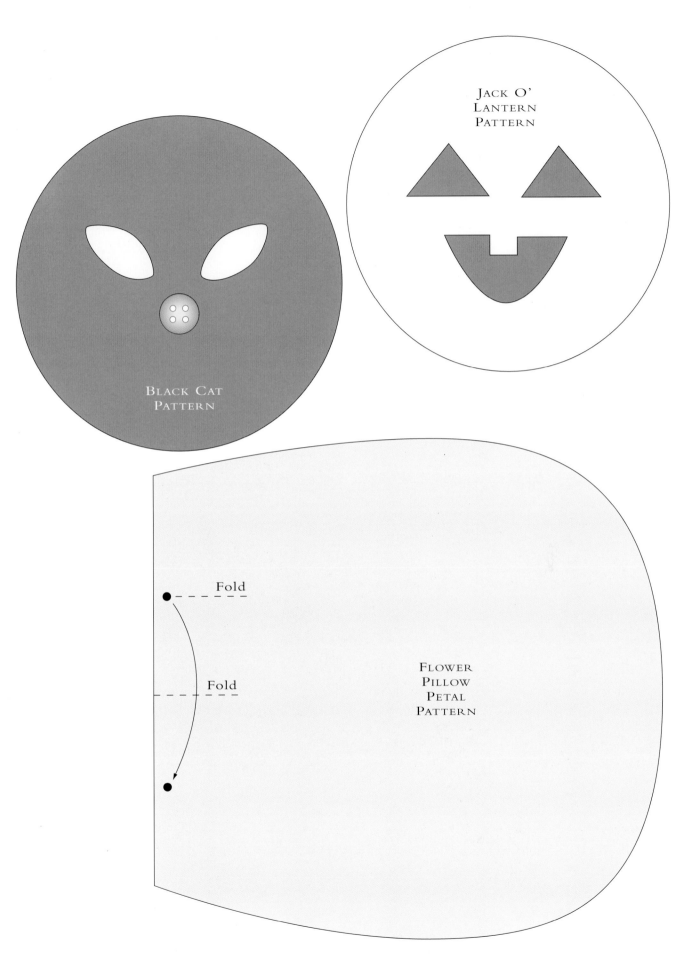

JACK O'
LANTERN
PATTERN

BLACK CAT
PATTERN

Fold

Fold

FLOWER
PILLOW
PETAL
PATTERN

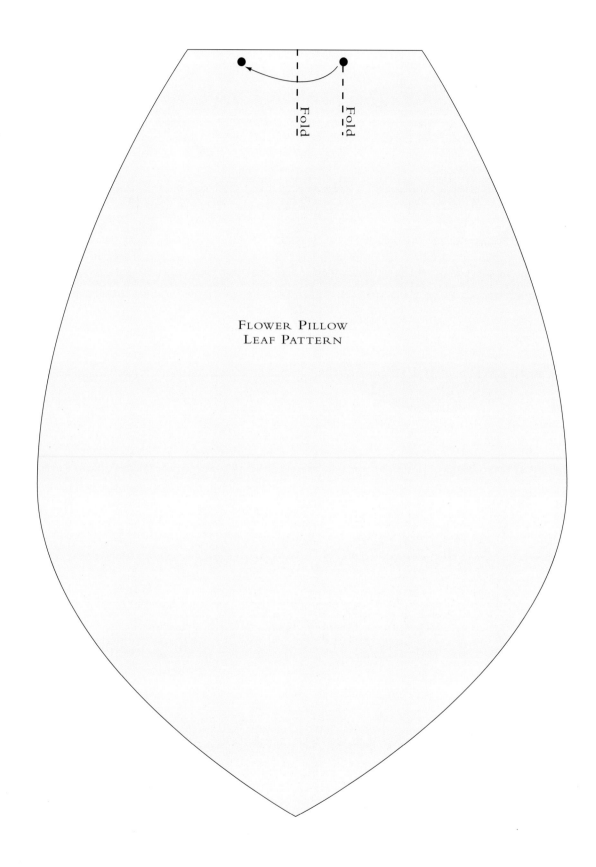

Fold

Fold

FLOWER PILLOW
LEAF PATTERN

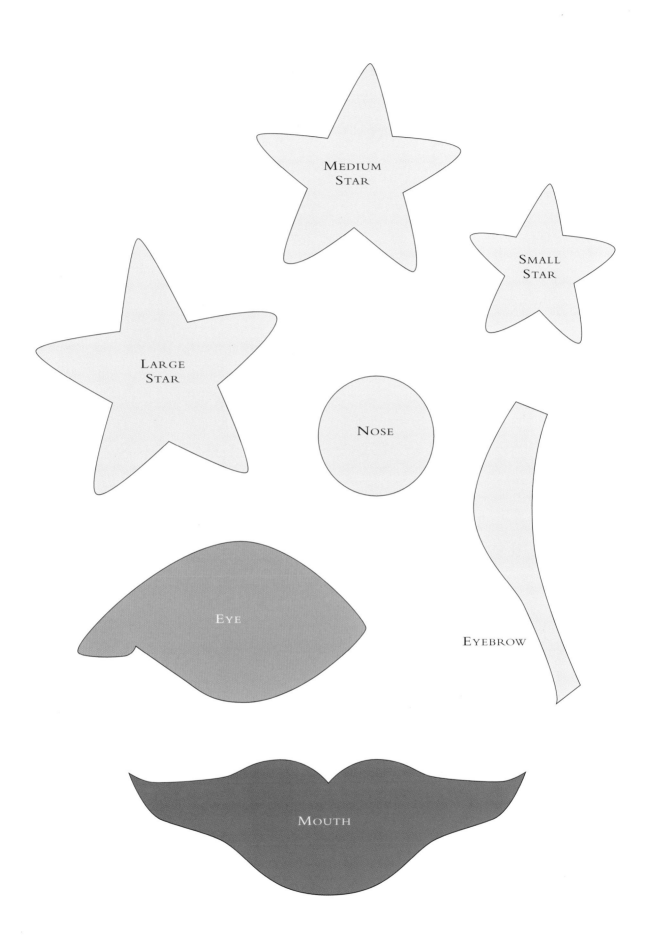

MEDIUM
STAR

SMALL
STAR

LARGE
STAR

NOSE

EYEBROW

EYE

MOUTH

Connect with right side of clouds

Cloud Pattern

Left Side

Enlarge 150% on copy machine

CLOUD PATTERN

Right Side

Enlarge 150% on
copy machine

Connect with left side of
clouds

Merry Nader

MERRY NADER'S DESIGNS

Merry Nader interprets the four seasons in a quartet of designer bags. For autumn, the Harvest Moon backpack is a great all-purpose tote, especially suited for carrying books to school in style!

Fill the Snowman Tote with gifts and treats when visiting friends and family during the winter holidays. The crazy-patch front is fun and easy, and provides lots of room for creative colorful embroidery.

Celebrate spring with the charming Easter bag and hat for a favorite little girl.

And for the long lazy days of summer, Merry created a light, airy purse with delicate bullion-stitch embroidery, and you can almost hear the bees buzzing!

Autumn: Harvest Moon Backpack

Finished size 16" x 18"

MATERIALS

- ⅞ yard of brown plaid fleece for pack and handles
- ¾ yard of coordinating fabric for lining
- 7" scrap of gold wool fabric for appliqué
- Orange, green, gold, and brown pearl cotton
- 28 assorted buttons
- 3 assorted charms
- Small bird button
- Black seed beeds
- Clear seed beads
- Beading needle
- Beading thread
- Silver quilter's pencil (optional)

CUTTING

1. From the brown plaid fleece, cut two 17½" x 21½" rectangles. Cut two 4" x 39" strips for the straps.
2. From the lining fabric, cut two 17½" x 21½" rectangles.
3. From the gold wool scrap, cut a 6" circle for the moon appliqué.

SUMMER

WINTER

AUTUMN

SPRING

Slit

DIAGRAM A

DIAGRAM B

1. Position the moon on the right side of one of the fleece rectangles, and appliqué using pearl cotton and a blanket stitch.

2. Referring to the photo as needed, back-stitch the words "Harvest Moon" with pearl cotton. Use a stem stitch to make the pumpkins, and chain stitch and feather stitch to make the tree. If desired, use the silver quilter's pencil to lightly write the words and to sketch the pumpkins and tree branches before you begin stitching. When the stitching is completed, rub away any remaining pencil marks. Hand-stitch a small bird button to a branch where it crosses the moon.

3. Make a 3"-long slit in the center of the second fleece rectangle, ¾" down from the top edge. See Diagram A. Sew a narrow zigzag stitch along both cut edges.

4. Place the front and back rectangles right sides together. Starting at the top edge on each side, sew down the side and part-way across the bottom, leaving a 5"-wide opening in the center of the bottom edge. Use a ¼" seam allowance. See Diagram B. Do not turn the bag right side out.

5. Sew the 4" x 39" strips together to make one long strip. Fold the strip in half lengthwise, right sides together, and sew along the long side. Turn the tube right side out. Fold the strip in half cross-wise, and mark the center with a pin.

6. To add the straps, you must work on both sides of the bag at the same time. The straps are placed on the wrong side (the inside) of the bag, but the pins must be on the right side (the outside) of the bag so that they can be removed later. Using safety pins, add the straps as follows: Match the center of the strap to the center front of the bag on the wrong side. Pin the strap so that the top edge is about 2" down from the top raw edge of the bag. Smoothing the straps as you go, pin every few inches around the top edge of the bag. Be sure to pin from the right side of the bag. Keep the strap an equal distance from the top all the way around the bag. See Diagram C. Insert the two ends into the slit at the back of the bag; pin the straps at the edge of the opening.

7. Turn the bag right side out. Smooth the straps down the center back of the bag; add a few pins to hold them in place. Turn the bag wrong side out again, and gently pull the ends of the straps through the seam opening at the bottom of the bag. Pin the ends about 1½" apart in the opening. Sew the seam closed, securing the strap ends at the same time. Trim the strap ends even with the seam allowance.

8. Place the lining rectangles right sides together, and stitch around three sides using a ¼" seam allowance. Place the lining inside the bag, right sides together, and sew around the top edge, leaving an opening for turning. Turn the bag right side out through the opening; slip-stitch the opening closed.

9. Tuck the lining inside the bag, and hand-tack the bottom edge in a few places to

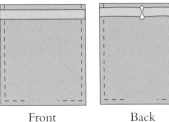

Front   Back

DIAGRAM C

secure the lining. Topstitch by hand or machine around the top of the bag below the straps, about 3½" inches from the top edge. Be sure to stitch through both layers. Remove the pins holding the straps in place.

FINISHING

1. Thread a beading needle with about 18" of beading thread and tie a small knot in the end. Insert the needle into the fleece at one bottom corner of the bag, right next to the bottom seam. Thread about 30 black seed beads onto the needle; the number does not have to be exact. (The beaded strands on the bag shown are about 2" long; make them all the same length or vary the lengths as desired.)

2. At the end of the line of beads, loop the thread through one hole of a button. Then, carefully thread the needle back up

through the beads; it is important to go through every one of them. See Diagram D. Gently tug on the button to pull any slack out of the thread; the top bead should be right against the fleece.

3. Insert the needle back into the fleece, and come out again about ½" away from the first strand. Repeat the process, threading the beads, adding the button, then coming back up through the beads and into the fleece. Remember to gently pull the slack out each time. Repeat every ½" across the bottom of the bag, starting a new thread as needed.

4. In the same manner, use the clear seed beads to accent the top of the bag. Thread five strands ranging from 1¼" to 2½" long, adding a button or charm at the end of each one.

DIAGRAM D

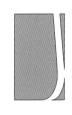

Winter: Snowman Tote Bag

Finished size 15" x 16"

ASSEMBLY

1. To make a pattern for the bag, cut a 15" x 16" rectangle from freezer paper. Fold the paper in half lengthwise, and mark a line to round off the bottom corner as shown in Diagram E. Use a plate to mark the curve or draw it free-hand. Taper the sides slightly so that the top is narrower than the bottom. This gives the bag a graceful shape. Trim the pattern along the marked lines.

2. Unfold the paper pattern, and use it to cut one bag back from the red plaid fleece. Use the pattern to cut three pieces from the lining fabric: a back, a front, and a foundation for the patchwork.

3. Trace the snowman pattern on page 85 onto a piece of gray fleece. Referring to the photo and the pattern as needed, embroider the snowman patch. Referring to the photo, pin the snowman patch to the foundation piece.

4. Building around the snowman patch,

MATERIALS

- ¾ yard of red plaid fleece for back and straps

- 1 yard of fabric for lining and crazy-patch foundation

- Scraps of gray, red, blue, green, and white fleece for patches

- Freezer paper or other large paper for pattern

cut and pin fleece scraps in the color, size, and shape of your choice, with edges butting together or overlapping slightly. Stitch the patches to the background using a tiny zigzag stitch and clear nylon thread.

5. Embroider the seams and the patches as desired. Patterns for several of the patches are provided on pages 85–87; copy these stitches or design your own combinations. To create the candy-cane stripes used for the words "Let It Snow,"

DIAGRAM E

position one color of pearl cotton, then couch it down with the second color of pearl cotton, angling the stitches slightly.

6. Place the bag front and bag back right sides together; stitch around three sides using a ¼" seam allowance.

7. To make the straps, cut two 4" x 30" strips from the red plaid fleece. Fold the strips in half lengthwise, right sides together, and stitch the long side. Turn the tube right side out. Position one strap on the right side of the bag front, with the ends approximately 4½" apart. Match the raw ends of the straps with the top raw edge of the bag; pin and baste in position. In the same manner,

pin the second strap to the right side of the bag back.

8. Place the front and back lining pieces right sides together; stitch with a ¼" seam allowance.

9. Place the lining and the bag right sides together with the straps between the layers. Sew together around the top edge, leaving an opening for turning.

10. Turn the bag right side out through the opening; slipstitch the opening closed. Tuck the lining inside the bag, and hand-tack the bottom edge in a few places to hold the lining in place.

CUTTING

1. From the fleece, cut a bag front and a back using the pattern on page 88. Cut two 1½" x 15" straps. Cut one 1½"-wide strip to fit around the crown of the hat.

2. From the lining fabric, cut a front and back using the pattern.

3. From the fabric scraps, cut one flower, one flower center, and two leaves using the patterns on page 88. These are the purse appliqués. To prepare the hat appliqués, you need two pieces of each fabric scrap. Trace the flower, flower center, and two leaves onto the paper side of fusible web. Cut loosely around the shapes, and fuse to the wrong side of the chosen fabrics. Cut the shapes on the traced lines, and fuse each one to a matching piece of fabric, making a two-sided appliqué. Trim the second piece to match the shape of the first.

ASSEMBLY

1. Referring to the photo, use pearl cotton and a blanket stitch to appliqué the flower and leaves to the right side of the bag front.

2. Place the bag front and back right sides together; sew. Pin a strap to the front of the bag on the right side, matching the ends of the strap to the raw edge at the top of the bag. Pin the second strap to the bag back.

3. Pin the two lining pieces right sides together; stitch.

4. Put the lining and the bag right sides together with the straps between the layers. Sew around the top edge, leaving an opening for turning. Turn right side out through the opening, and slip-stitch the opening closed. Using pearl cotton, blanket-stitch along both edges of the straps.

5. Blanket-stitch along both long edges of the 1½"-wide hatband. Place the strip on the hat and hot-glue the ends in place. Blanket-stitch the flower center to the flower, then blanket-stitch around the edges of the flower and the leaves. Hot-glue the flower and leaf appliqués to the front of the hat.

ASSEMBLY

1. Trace the pattern on page 89 and use it to cut two bag pieces from the fleece and two lining pieces from the cotton.

2. Referring to the photo and the pattern as needed, embroider one of the fleece pieces using pearl cotton. The sunflower "petals" and the bee bodies are made from bullion stitches; the leaves are feather stitches outlined with stem stitch; the flower centers are French knots.

3. Place the bag front and back right sides together, and stitch with a ¼" seam allowance. Stitch the lining pieces together in the same manner.

4. Place the bag and the lining right sides together; stitch around the top edge, leaving an opening for turning.

MATERIALS

- ¼ yard of white fleece for bag

- ¼ yard of cotton print fabric for lining

- Blue, black, brown, yellow, gray, and green pearl cotton

- 1¼ yards of ¼" white decorative cord

Turn the bag right side out through the opening; slip-stitch the opening closed.

5. Tuck the lining inside the bag. If desired, add a few tiny handstitches along the inside bottom of the bag to secure the lining.

6. Use pearl cotton to hand-stitch a ¼"-long blanket stitch around the outside edge. Stitch the ends of the cord just inside the top edge of the bag.

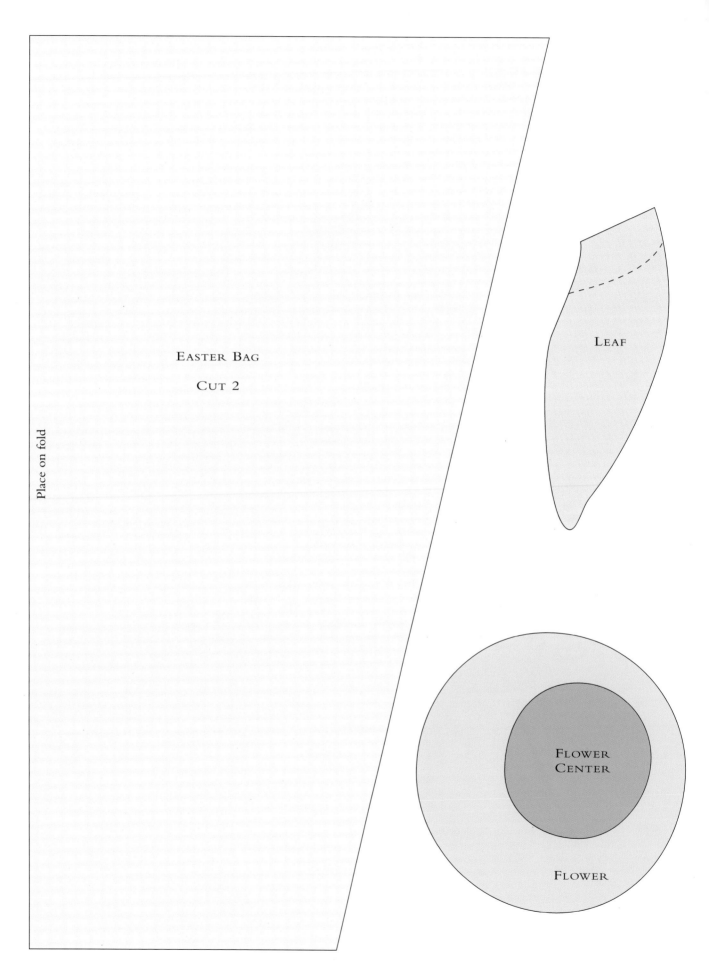

EASTER BAG

CUT 2

Place on fold

LEAF

FLOWER CENTER

FLOWER

Janis Bullis

CREATIVE SERVICES

To ward off the autumn chill, red fleece and elegant trims are warm, comfy, and stylish! Janis Bullis transformed a purchased pattern into a boutique look. Look for unusual laces, braids, beads, and other trims to embellish your vest for an ethnic look.

Holiday stockings are fun to make, and this one features jingle bells to alert eager ears when the jolly old elf arrives. Beaded and sequined snowflakes drift softly down the front of the stocking, making it suitable for a child or grown-up of any age.

For spring, Janis thought bright pink, pale blue, pretty pastel flowers…and came up with comfy slippers for a child. Several sizes are included with the pattern and with so many interesting button styles to choose from now, let your creativity soar.

Summer and vacations are synonymous. Since Janis loves to go to the beach with a lot of good books, she designed this bag to hold plenty of the essentials—towel, books, lotion, plus a bit more!

Autumn: Ethnic Vest

MATERIALS

- Purchased vest pattern★
- Red fleece yardage according to the pattern requirements (omit lining)
- ¼ yard of red lining fabric for collar
- 1½ yards of ⅜"-wide flat black lace
- 1½ yards of ¾"-wide flat black lace
- 5½ yards of ½"-wide foldover black braid
- Two 1" buttons
- 26 ½" flat beads for collar trim

★*Note:* The vest shown was made using McCall's Pattern #8699.

ASSEMBLY

1. From the fleece, cut the vest front, back, and one pair of collar pieces. From the lining fabric, cut one pair of collar pieces.
2. Trim the seam allowance from all sides except the collar, front neckline, shoulder, and side seams.
3. Stitch the curved edge of each collar piece to its matching lining piece. Trim the seam, and turn to the right side. Referring to the photo, use a narrow zigzag stitch to sew two rows of lace to the collar, the ⅜"-wide lace toward the inside and the ¾"-wide lace on the outside edge.

SUMMER

WINTER

AUTUMN

SPRING

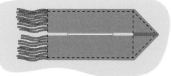

DIAGRAM A

4. Stitch the collar to the vest front having the right side of the collar facing the wrong side of the vest. Clip the seams and grade the seam allowance to reduce bulk. Stitch through the seam allowance and the vest front a scant ¼" from the first line of stitching to prevent the seam from creeping around to the front.

5. Sew the shoulder seams. Grade the seam allowance and stitch the seam as you did in Step 4.

6. Cut two 18" lengths of braid for the back ties. Pin them into the side seams 4" up from the bottom edge of the vest. Stitch the side seams.

7. Bind the raw edges with foldover braid. Cut two 6" lengths of the braid; fold and stitch each piece at the buttonhole placement as shown in Diagram A. Stitch the beads to the collar.

···

Winter: Snowflake Stocking

20" long

CUTTING

1. From the green fleece, cut one stocking and one reverse stocking using the pattern on pages 97-100. From the lining fabric, cut one stocking and one reverse stocking. Cut a 3" x 9" piece of the lining fabric for a hanger.

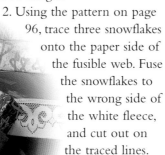

2. Using the pattern on page 96, trace three snowflakes onto the paper side of the fusible web. Fuse the snowflakes to the wrong side of the white fleece, and cut out on the traced lines.

ASSEMBLY

1. Fuse the snowflakes to the front of the stocking, placing the highest snowflake about 8" from the top raw edge. Allow for ½" seams on the sides when positioning the snowflakes. Using a double strand of thread, sew a snowflake sequin and bead to the center and around the outer edges of each snowflake.

2. With right sides together and using a ½" seam allowance, stitch a

MATERIALS

- ½ yard of green fleece
- ½ yard of lining fabric
- ¼ yard of white fleece for snowflakes
- Fusible web
- Twenty-one 1" red, green, and gold snowflake sequins with hole
- Twenty-one 6mm clear faceted beads
- Twenty-four ½" jingle bells for cuff

fleece stocking piece to a lining piece along the top edge, as shown in Diagram B. Repeat with the second fleece piece and lining piece.

Lining (ws)

DIAGRAM B

3. Place the two stocking/lining units right sides together as shown in Diagram C, and stitch all the way around, leaving an opening in the lining for turning. Clip curves and turn the stocking right side

out through the opening; stitch the opening closed. Slip the lining down inside the fleece stocking and topstitch ¼" from the upper edge of the stocking.

4. To make the hanging tab, fold the 3" x 9" piece of lining fabric in half lengthwise with wrong sides together; press. Open up the piece and fold the side edges into the center crease; press. See Diagram D. Bring the folded edges together, and topstitch along the edge with the double folds. Fold the tab in half crosswise and stitch to the inside of the stocking where indicated on the pattern piece.

5. Fold the cuff down and sew the jingle bells to the lower edge of the cuff.

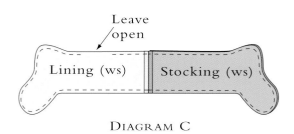

Leave open

Lining (ws)   Stocking (ws)

DIAGRAM C

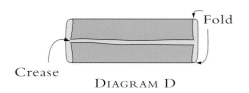

Fold

Crease

DIAGRAM D

<hr>

Spring: Cozy Slippers

MATERIALS

for child's slippers★

- ¼ yard of light blue fleece for child's slippers
- ½ yard of blue print prequilted fabric for lining
- Two 6" x 11" pieces of Jiffy Grip fabric for child's soles
- ⅜ yard of heavyweight interfacing
- Decorative buttons
- ¼ yard of ¼"-wide elastic (optional)

★Note: Child's Medium is approximately size 1.

CUTTING

1. For each pair of slippers, cut two sides and two reverse sides from the fleece using the patterns on pages 101-103. Transfer the dots from the patterns to the fabric pieces.

2. From the prequilted lining fabric, cut two sides and two reverse sides for each pair. Cut two soles and four tabs.

2. Cut two soles from the Jiffy Grip fabric and two soles from the interfacing for each pair.

ASSEMBLY

1. Baste one interfacing sole to the wrong side of one lining sole using a ¼" seam allowance.

2. With right sides together, pin and stitch the lining sides at the center back, and at the center front from the dot to the toe. Matching the dots on the soles to the seams, and with right sides together, pin and stitch the lining sole to the lining sides. See Diagram E. Leave a 2" to 3" opening along one side edge for turning. Trim seams and clip curves.

3. Repeat Step 2, substituting fleece sides and Jiffy Grip soles. The "pebbled" side of the Jiffy Grip is the right side of the fabric. Do not leave an opening for turning.

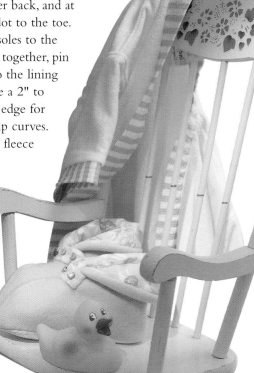

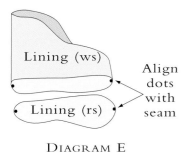

Lining (ws)

Lining (rs)

Align dots with seam

DIAGRAM E

4. With right sides facing, stitch the fleece slipper to the quilted slipper at the cuff edge, starting and ending at the V. Trim and clip the seam allowances. Turn the slipper to the right side through the opening.

5. If you wish, cut a 3" length of elastic. Stitch each end of the elastic to the wrong side of the slipper underneath the point of the V. For a snug, comfortable fit, stretch the elastic slightly while stitching.

6. With right sides together, stitch around the edges of the tab pieces, leaving a small opening for turning. Turn, hand-stitch the opening closed, and press flat.

7. Center the tab over the point of the V on the fleece side of the slipper, and hand-stitch the short blunt end in place over the elastic. Reverse the direction of the tab for the other slipper. Sew a button to the pointed end of the tab to attach it to the slipper. Add buttons as desired.

Summer: Sailboat Tote

16" x 18"

CUTTING

1. From the blue fleece, cut four 3" x 17" strips for the top, two 4" x 17" strips for the base, and one 7¼" x 9 ½" rectangle for the pocket. Cut one floor using the oval pattern on page 105.

2. From the white fleece, cut two 14" x 17" pieces for the sides. Cut one hull, one large sail, and one small sail using the patterns on page 104.

3. From the lining fabric, cut two 17" x 19" pieces for the sides, and cut one floor using the oval pattern.

4. From the cardboard, cut one floor using the oval pattern.

ASSEMBLY

1. With right sides together and all edges even, stitch the long edges of the white fleece sides to the long edges of the blue fleece bases. Stitch the blue fleece top pieces to the top edge of the white fleece sides. Matching seams, stitch the side seams to make a tube. Use ½" seam allowances throughout.

2. Stitch the short sides of the two remaining blue fleece top pieces. Stitch this unit to the top edge of the unit from Step 1 as shown in Diagram F. Press to the inside to create a facing.

MATERIALS

- ½ yard of navy blue fleece for tote and pocket
- ½ yard of white fleece for tote
- 1¼ yards of 45"-wide white cotton fabric for lining
- 10" x 14" heavyweight fusible interfacing
- 3½ yards of ½" cotton cable cord
- 1 yard of ⅛" cotton cable cord
- Scraps of blue rickrack and yellow ribbon
- Purchased star and anchor appliqués
- Twelve ⅛" and twenty-four ⁷⁄₁₆" silver grommets
- 10" x 14" cardboard
- Eyelet application tool
- Tacky fabric glue

3. Mark the position of the eyelets in the base pieces as shown in Diagram G. Apply six $\frac{7}{16}$" eyelets each to the front and back base.

4. Apply interfacing to the wrong side of the fleece floor. Matching dots to the seams, stitch the floor to the sides.

5. Cut a 1-yard length of the $\frac{1}{2}$" cord. Weave the cord through the eyelets in the base and knot the ends on the inside of the tote.

6. For the lining, stitch together the 17" edges, with right sides together and raw edges even. Matching dots to seams, stitch the lining floor to the sides.

7. With wrong sides facing, insert the lining in the tote. Pin and baste the lining to the fleece sides at the top edges, underneath the facing.

8. Turn under $\frac{1}{2}$" on the lower edge of the facing and hand-stitch to the sides through the lining. Mark the position of the eyelets in the top as in Step 3 and Diagram G. Apply six $\frac{7}{16}$" eyelets each to the front and back. Beginning and ending at the center front, weave the remaining $\frac{1}{2}$" cord through the eyelets at the top. Tie the ends into a small bow.

9. Stitch a $\frac{1}{4}$" hem in one short edge of the pocket. Mark eyelet positions $\frac{1}{2}$" in from the edge and every 2" around the other three sides of the pocket. Apply the small eyelets to the pocket. Beginning and ending at the top edge, weave the narrow cord through the eyelets and tie a knot at each end.

10. Apply glue to the wrong side of the sailboat pieces and glue them to the pocket. Apply glue to the side and lower edges of the pocket and glue it to the front of the tote. Cut a 3" piece of yellow ribbon and fold it in half with a dab of glue inside. Cut a notch in the ends and glue the ribbon to the main sail. Cut rickrack to decorate the mast and boat. Glue the rickrack on along with the purchased appliqués. Place a large book over the pocket on a flat surface, and allow to dry.

11. Trim $\frac{1}{2}$" from all edges of the cardboard floor. Insert the cardboard floor into the tote.

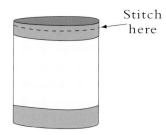

Stitch here

DIAGRAM F

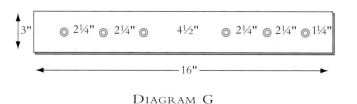

3" | 2¼" | 2¼" | 4½" | 2¼" | 2¼" | 1¼"

16"

DIAGRAM G

SNOWFLAKE PATTERN

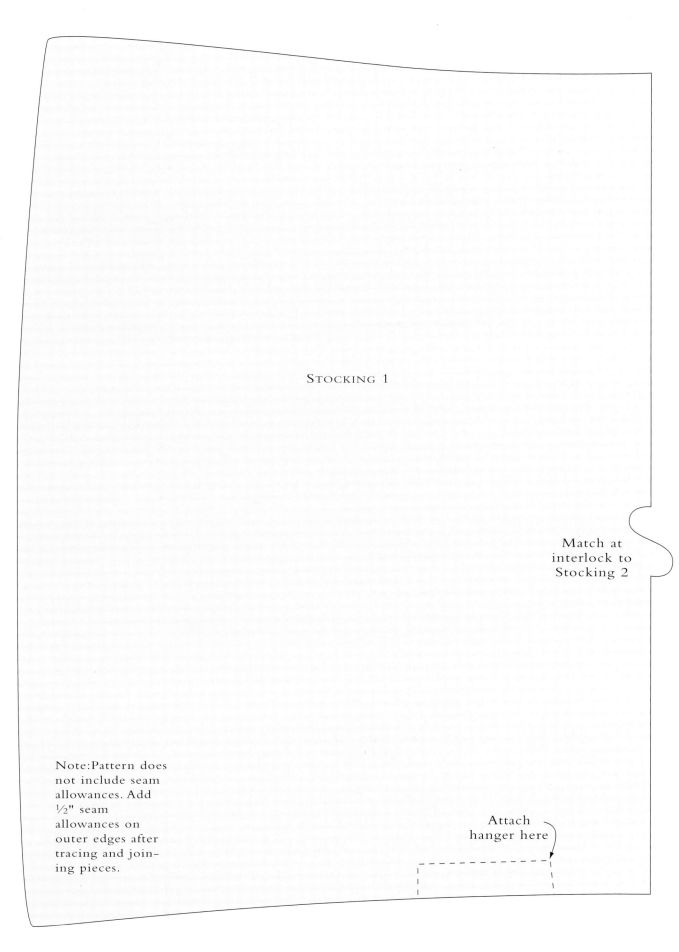

STOCKING 1

Match at
interlock to
Stocking 2

Note:Pattern does
not include seam
allowances. Add
½" seam
allowances on
outer edges after
tracing and join-
ing pieces.

Attach
hanger here

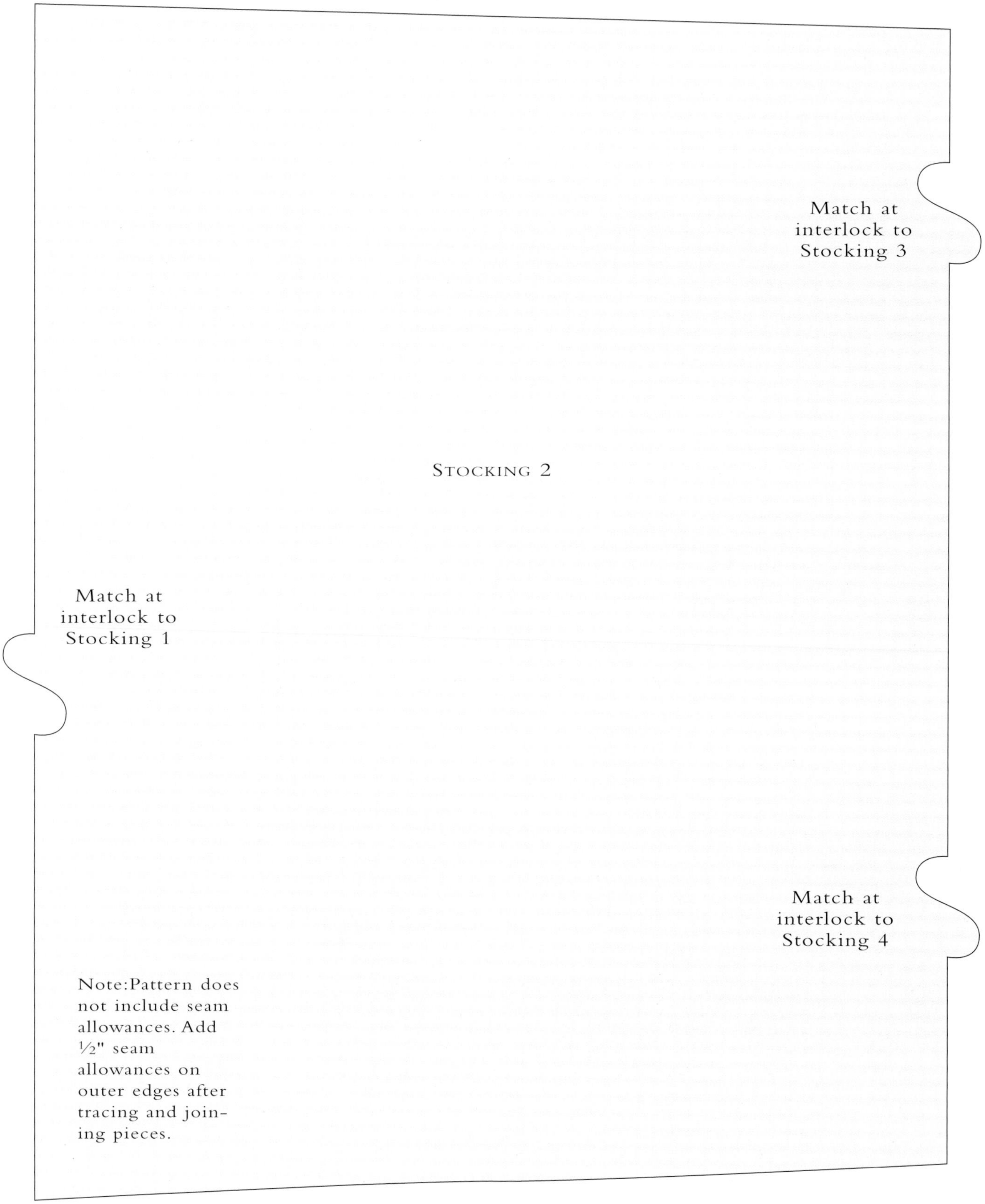

Match at
interlock to
Stocking 3

STOCKING 2

Match at
interlock to
Stocking 1

Match at
interlock to
Stocking 4

Note:Pattern does
not include seam
allowances. Add
½" seam
allowances on
outer edges after
tracing and join-
ing pieces.

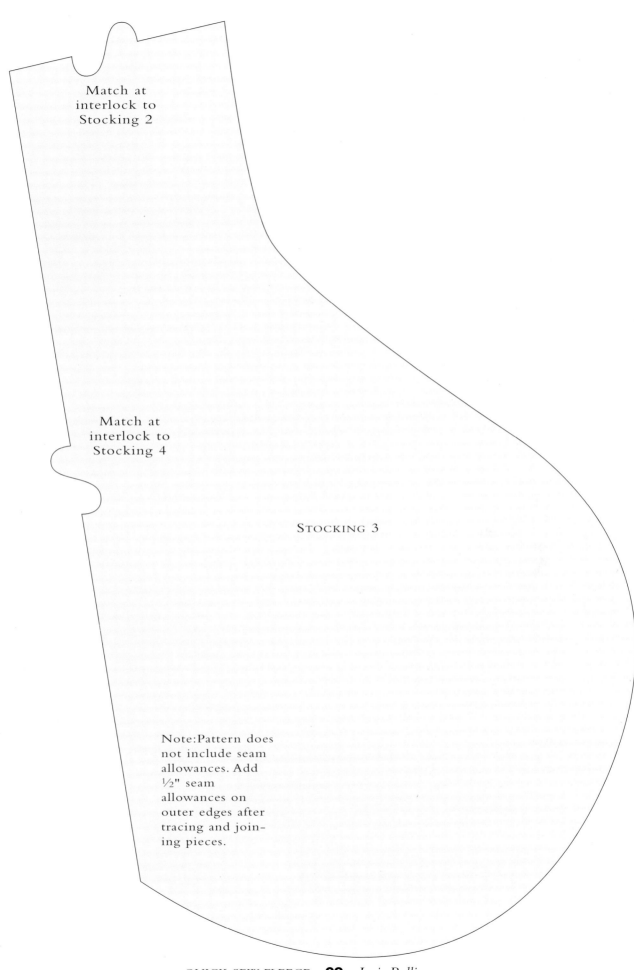

Match at
interlock to
Stocking 2

Match at
interlock to
Stocking 4

STOCKING 3

Note:Pattern does
not include seam
allowances. Add
½" seam
allowances on
outer edges after
tracing and join-
ing pieces.

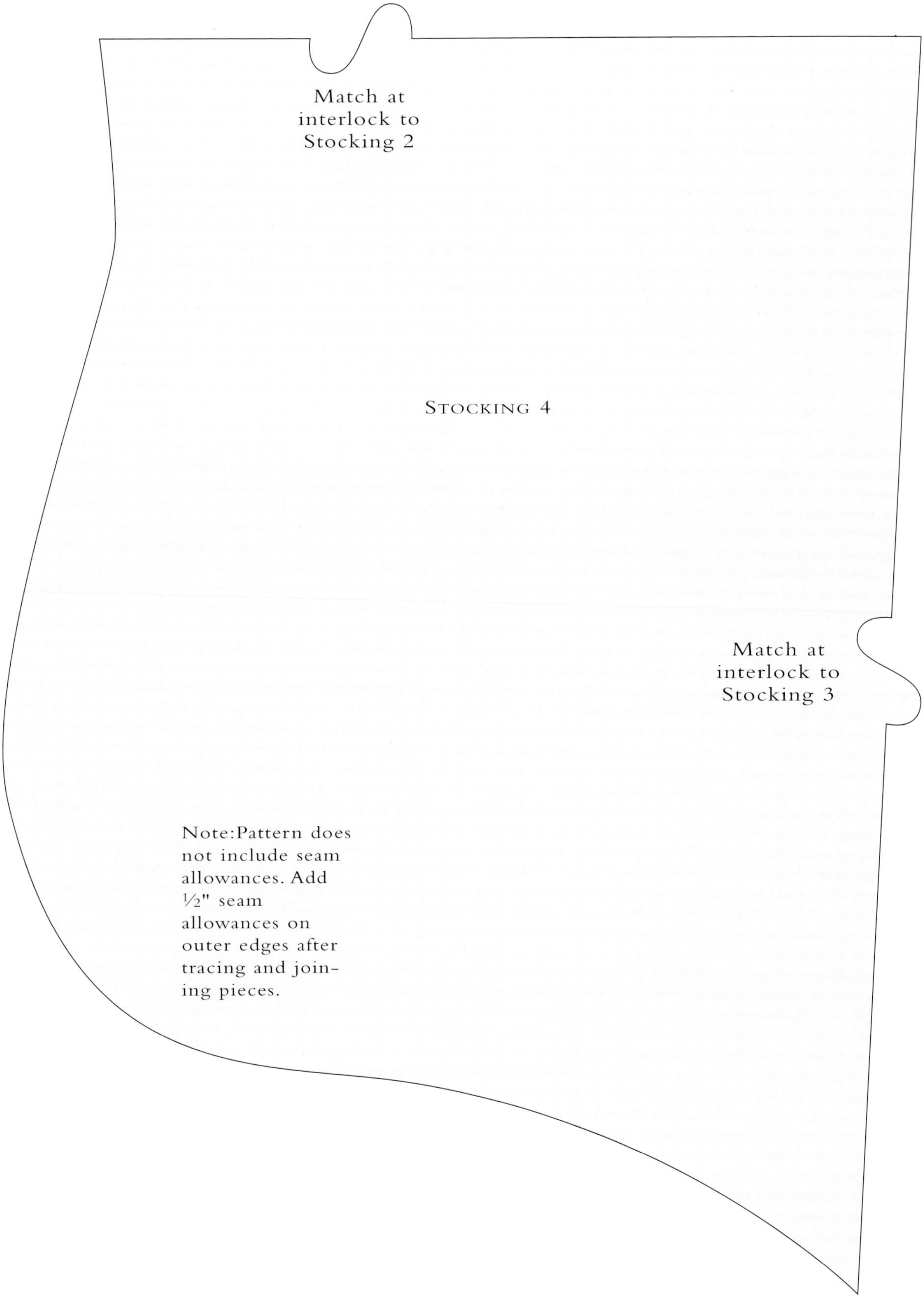

Match at
interlock to
Stocking 2

STOCKING 4

Match at
interlock to
Stocking 3

Note:Pattern does
not include seam
allowances. Add
½" seam
allowances on
outer edges after
tracing and join-
ing pieces.

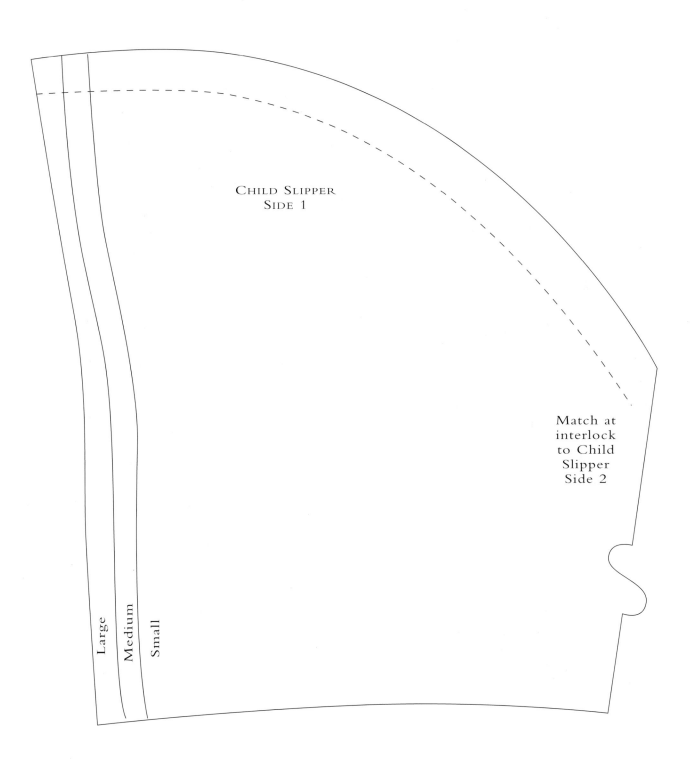

CHILD SLIPPER
SIDE 1

Match at
interlock
to Child
Slipper
Side 2

Large

Medium

Small

CHILD SLIPPER TAB

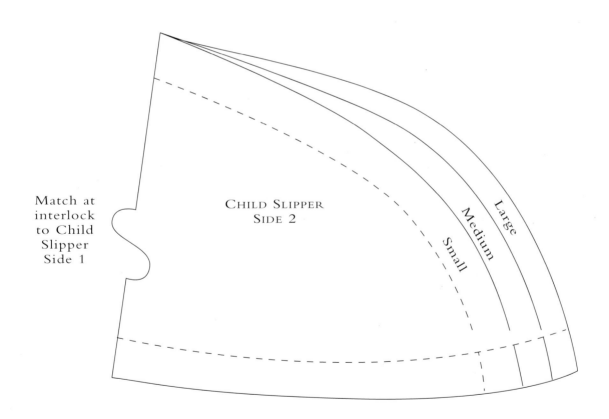

Match at interlock to Child Slipper Side 1

CHILD SLIPPER SIDE 2

Small

Medium

Large

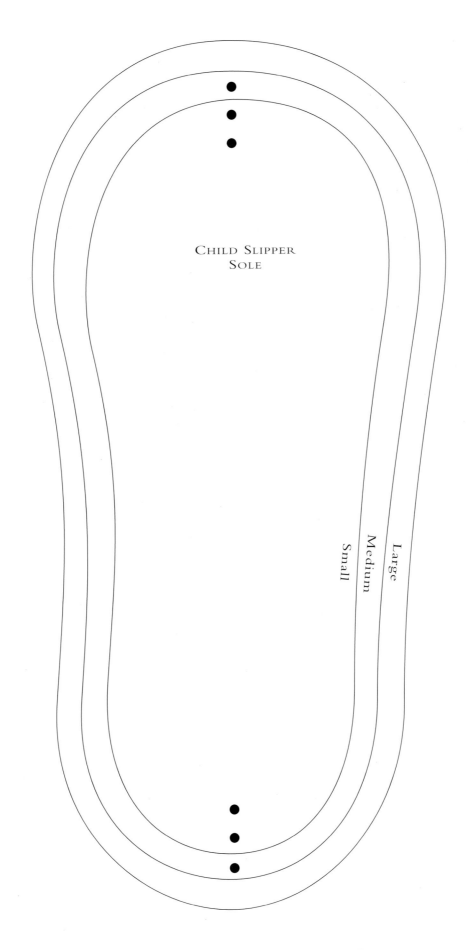

CHILD SLIPPER
SOLE

Small

Medium

Large

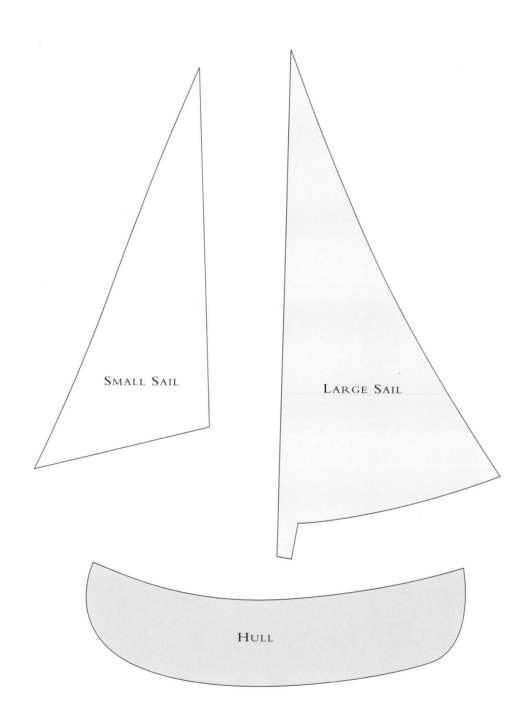

SMALL SAIL

LARGE SAIL

HULL

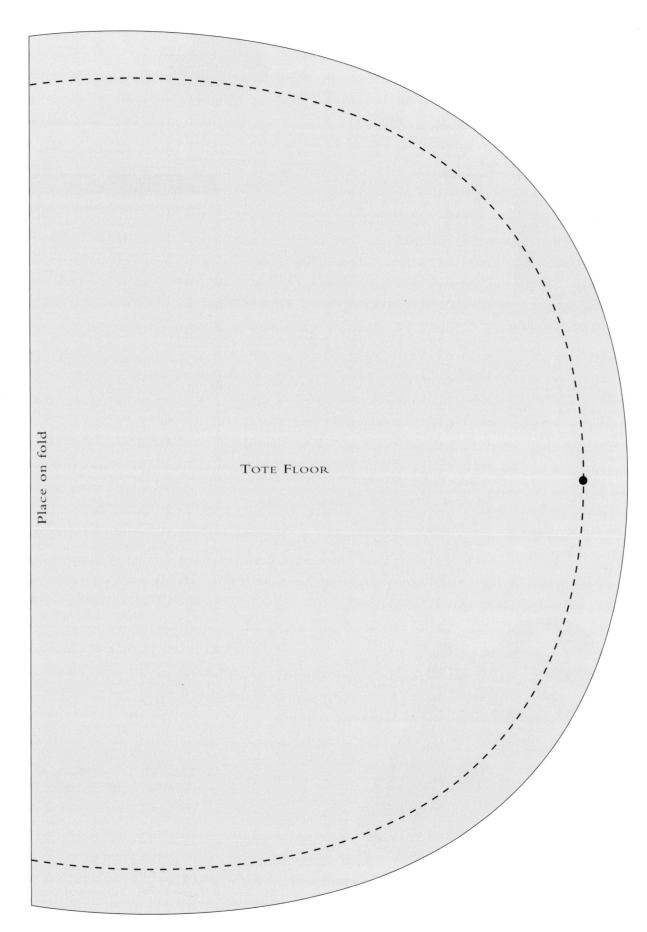

Place on fold

TOTE FLOOR

Mary Mulari

MARY'S PRODUCTIONS

F leece is so versatile, it's easy to think of dozens of ways to use it. And Mary Mulari has done just that!

Whatever the outdoor spectator sport, when chilling autumn winds start to blow, the Tailgate Tote has a handy pocket to carry your program and ticket stubs, plus once at your seat in the metal bleachers, it unbuttons into a padded cushion and a cozy blanket to wrap up in.

The fleece Polar Prince and Princess are a delightful duo that children and adults alike will enjoy. Sensibly dressed for cold weather in mittens, boots, hat, and scarf, this whimsical wintertime pair will be a cheerful sight on a chair or fireplace mantel.

Everyone's ready for a burst of color when spring arrives. And Mary's fun and funky Kids Hats are just the ticket for welcoming the new season. They're so much fun that kids won't even mind wearing a hat! And they couldn't be easier to make.

As you pack for summer vacation, once again fleece fits right in. It cushions and protects bottles from breakage, is lightweight, and launders easily. With Mary's terrific Travel Tote Trio you can carry the neckroll pillow and the half-circle bag in the large tote. Stuff a scarf or clothing into the neckroll for an instant pillow for car or airplane. Stash cosmetics or other small items into the handy zippered half-circle bag.

Autumn: Tailgate Tote

MATERIALS

- 1 yard of 60"-wide plaid fleece for blanket
- ½ yard of green fleece for pocket and cushion
- ½ yard of purple fleece for cushion
- 5 yards of 1½"-wide grosgrain ribbon
- 4 buttons
- 18" x 20" piece of 1" thick foam

CUTTING

1. From the green fleece, cut two 18" x 20" rectangles; one for the pocket and the other for one side of the cushion.
2. From the purple fleece, cut one 18" x 20" rectangle for one side of the cushion.
3. Do not cut the plaid fleece. Simply square it up by trimming any uneven edges. On each short edge, cut fringe ¼" apart, 3½" deep.

ASSEMBLY

1. Cut two pieces of ribbon, each 11" long. Fold under 3½" on one end of each ribbon and topstitch in place. Place the ribbons on a green 18" x 20" rectangle so that the folded-under sections extend beyond the edge of the cushion top. See Diagram A. Pin in place.
2. Topstitch the ribbons to the fleece, stopping ½" from the edge to allow for seam allowance. See Diagram B.

SUMMER

WINTER

AUTUMN

SPRING

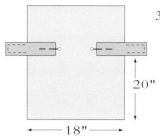

DIAGRAM A

18" — 20"

DIAGRAM B

3. Cut one piece of ribbon 50" long. Fold under 2" on each edge and topstitch in place. Referring to Diagram C, pin the ribbon to the fleece to form a handle. The ribbons should be 3½" in from the edges, with the 2" folded tabs extending beyond the bottom edge of the rectangle. Stitch the the ribbon in place, again stopping stitching ½" away from each edge to allow for seam allowances.

4. Work a buttonhole in each ribbon extension, again referring to Diagram C.

5. Fold the ribbon handle and buttonhole extensions back and pin them to the right side of the green fleece, out of the way of the seam allowance. Layer the purple rectangle over the green fleece, right sides together. Stitch the cushion pieces together using a ½" seam allowance, leaving an opening for turning at the bottom.

6. Turn the cushion right side out and insert the foam rectangle. Stitch the opening closed.

7. To make the pocket, fold the other green rectangle in half so it measures 18" x 10". Serge or clean finish the three sides with raw edges. Turn under the serged edges and pin to the blanket, referring to Diagram D for correct placement. Topstitch the pocket in place.

8. Cut a 47" length of ribbon, and turn under ½" on each end. Topstitch the ribbon to the pocket, placing the ribbon in 3½" from each side of the pocket as shown in Diagram E.

9. Stitch the four buttons to the ribbon handle on the pocket so they align with the buttonholes on the cushion. Fold the blanket and button the cushion to the blanket side.

Buttonholes

DIAGRAM C

16"
21" — 21"
10"

DIAGRAM D

DIAGRAM E

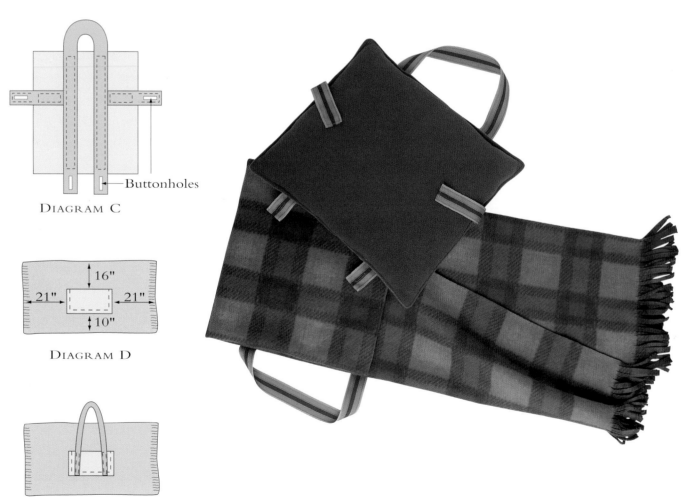

MATERIALS

- ⅔ yard of cream or white fleece for bodies
- ½ yard of red fleece for princess outfit
- Purple, black, gold, and gray fleece scraps for accessories
- 1¼ yards of ¼"-wide decorative trim for skirt
- White felt scraps for mitten trim
- Polyester stuffing
- Doll hair or yarn to make hair
- Eight curtain weights
- Four small black snaps
- Assorted ¼" buttons
- ¼ yard of ¼"-wide elastic
- Pom-pom
- 12" length of white or cream yarn
- Powder blush
- Two gold tinsel pipe cleaners

CUTTING

1. From the cream or white fleece, for each doll cut two doll bodies, two doll arms, and four doll legs using the patterns on pages 114–115.
2. From the red fleece, cut four mittens for each doll using the pattern provided. For the skirt and top, first trace the pattern pieces on pages 116–117 onto a folded piece of paper to make a full-size pattern of each piece. Then place the patterns on folded red fleece and cut out each garment piece according to the instructions on the pattern.

3. Use the pattern provided to cut four boots for each doll from the black fleece. For the prince, cut a 2½" x 24" strip of purple fleece for the scarf, and cut a 4½" x 9" piece of gray fleece for the hat. For the princess, cut a 2½" x 24" strip of gold fleece for the scarf, and cut a 4½" x 9" piece for the hat.

ASSEMBLY

1. Sew the arms and legs right sides together using a ⅛" seam allowance. Turn all four pieces right side out.
2. Pin the arms and legs to the right side of one body piece, in the positions indicated on the pattern. See Diagram F. Sew in place, stitching close to the edge.
3. Pin the second body piece on top of the first one and sew around, leaving an opening on one side as shown in Diagram G.
4. To create a flat bottom on the body, fold the lower corner as shown in Diagram H, matching the side and bottom seams. Stitch across the fold. Repeat on the other corner. Turn the body right side out through the opening.
5. Place the curtain weights in the bottom of the body and stuff the body. Hand-stitch the opening closed. Sew three buttons down the center front of the body. Repeat Steps 1 through 5 to make the second doll.
6. Sew the mittens and the boots right sides together, stitching around each pair with a ⅛" seam allowance. Turn all four pieces right side out. Repeat for the second pair.

FINISHING

1. For added details, cut two snowflakes from white felt and glue them in place on the mittens. (Fusing would flatten the fleece too much.) On the boots, use white yarn or thread to hand-sew five stitches across the top seams, creating the look of laces. Fit the mittens and the

DIAGRAM F

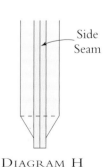

DIAGRAM G

Side Seam

DIAGRAM H

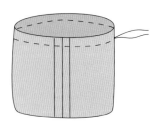

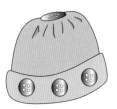

DIAGRAM I

boots onto the body. Turn under the top edge of the mittens, or trim the edge with pinking shears.

2. Tie the scarf around the doll's neck. Cut fringe ¼" apart, 1" deep into the ends of the scarf, if desired.

3. To make the hats, fold the 4½" x 9" gray fleece in half crosswise, right sides together. Sew across the short end using a ¼" seam allowance. Using a hand-sewing needle and doubled thread, gather one edge of the tube. Sew a button to the top of the gathering on the right side, or attach a yarn pom-pom. Turn up the opposite edge to form a cuff, and sew or glue an assortment of buttons around the cuff. Repeat for the gold hat, omitting the button trim. See Diagram I.

4. To dress the princess, zigzag stitch a 9" piece of elastic to the waist opening of the skirt. Decorate the hemline by stitching purchased trim in place.

5. For the princess top, trim the hemlines and sleeve ends with a pinking shears. Fold the top right sides together and stitch the underarm seams using a ¼" seam allowance. Turn right side out.

6. Glue or sew the hair to the head. Fit the hat over the head and hair, and arrange the hair as desired.

7. Hand-stitch two black snaps to the body for eyes. Give the dolls pink cheeks by brushing blush on the face with a cotton swab.

8. To form a magic wand, cut three pieces from the gold pipe cleaner: one 4" and two 1½" long. Twist the two short pieces around the longer piece, near the top. Cut two small slits in the palm of one mitten to insert the wand. Repeat for the second doll. Now, seat the prince and princess somewhere comfortable and watch them do their magic.

Spring: Adorable Hats

ASSEMBLY

1. From one color fleece, cut two front/back pieces and two side pieces using the patterns on pages 118-119. From a contrasting color fleece, cut hat brim pieces using the pattern. Trim the top edges of these pieces with pinking shears. Be sure to transfer the markings for the drawstring openings. If you prefer to make the hat from only one fabric, fit the pattern pieces together and cut each side as a single piece.

2. Place a hat brim section over each hat top section, overlapping ¼". See Diagram J. Pin, and sew the sections together using a regular straight stitch, or a blanket or other decorative stitch.

3. With right sides together, sew the bottom edge of the front and back sections. This forms the seam at the top center of the hat.

MATERIALS

■ ¼ yard each of two colors of fleece for hat

■ Assorted ribbon and buttons for trim (optional)

■ Scraps of tear-away stabilizer (optional)

4. Mark the center of the top edge of each side section. With right sides together, match and pin these marks to the seamline at the top center of the hat. Pin the "peaks" of each side section to the peaks on the front and back sections, then fit and pin along the remainder of each seam.

5. Sew the two continuous seams to form the hat. See Diagram K. Use a ¼" seam allowance, and backstitch at the end of each seam. If you have difficulty backstitching the top peaks, place a small piece of tear-away stabilizer under the

fabric ends and then carefully remove it after sewing.

6. To cut the openings for the drawstrings, slide a wooden block or small rotary cutting mat into the hat. Cut an opening at each mark using an eyelet cutter or buttonhole cutter. If you prefer, use scissors to carefully cut a small slit.

7. Cut a 32" length of ribbon or cording. Beginning in the center left hole on one side of the hat, lace the ribbon through the openings around the hat. A bodkin makes this process easier. Turn up the brim of the hat and tie the ends of the ribbon in a knot or bow. You can adjust how snugly the hat fits by pulling the ribbon more tightly before tying.

8. To "dress up" this simple hat, consider trimming it with a ribbon flower, a favorite pin from your jewelry box, or a sequined appliqué, or add buttons in between the ribbon segments. For changeable trims, pin them on instead of sewing them.

DIAGRAM J

DIAGRAM K

Summer: Travel Tote Trio

NECKROLL BAG/PILLOW

MATERIALS

- ⅓ yard of fleece for main pillow
- 6" x 12" piece of contrasting fleece for pillow ends
- 1⅓ yards of ribbon or cord for pillow drawstrings
- Twelve 1" daisy appliqués (optional)

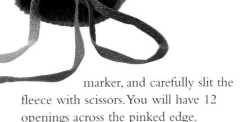

ASSEMBLY

1. Cut a 12" x 18" rectangle for the main pillow piece. From the same or a contrasting fleece, cut two 3" x 12" pillow end pieces. Trim one long edge of both pillow end pieces with pinking shears.

2. To cut openings for the drawstrings on the pillow end pieces, place a ruler ½" in from one short edge and ¾" from the pinked edge. See Diagram L. With a buttonhole cutter or eyelet cutter, cut an opening at the beginning of the ruler and at every inch mark. If you prefer, mark the openings with chalk or another marker, and carefully slit the fleece with scissors. You will have 12 openings across the pinked edge.

3. Fold the rectangle in half lengthwise, right sides together. Using a ¼" seam allowance, sew the rectangle into a tube. Turn right side out. Fold the end pieces in half crosswise, right sides together, and sew each into a tube. Leave these pieces inside out. See Diagram M.

4. With wrong sides together, fit the ends into the main pillow section as shown in Diagram N. Pin in place and sew around the ends with a ¼" seam allowance. Trim the seam allowances with pinking shears. With the ends still tucked inside the pillow, sew a second line of stitches 1"

½"

DIAGRAM L

DIAGRAM M

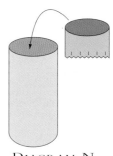

DIAGRAM N

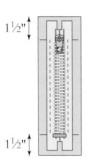

1½"

1½"

DIAGRAM P

Cut
here

Wrong
side of
fabric

DIAGRAM Q

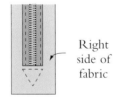

Right
side of
fabric

DIAGRAM R

Ribbon

DIAGRAM S

DIAGRAM O

from the first, forming a tuck at the edges of the pillow. See Diagram O.

5. Pull the ends out from inside the pillow. Thread the cord or ribbon through the openings around the pillow ends. Use a bodkin for speedy lacing through the openings.

6. Hand stitch the daisy appliqués in place, referring to the photograph for placement.

7. Stuff the pillow and pull the ties tight to tie bows. Less stuffing in the center of the pillow will make it easier for the pillow to bend around the neck.

HALF-CIRCLE BAG

MATERIALS

- ⅓ yard of fleece
- ⅛ yard of contrasting fleece
- 16" (or longer) contrasting color zipper
- 4" pieces of ribbon for zipper ends and/or handle
- Thread to match zipper or clear nylon thread
- 1¼" purchased monograms (optional)

ASSEMBLY

1. Cut out the bag using the pattern on page 120. Cut out the bag center strip from the same fabric or a contrasting fabric.

2. Center the zipper face up on the right side of the center fabric strip. Pin in place, pinning on both sides of the zipper tape. Mark the zipper tape 1½" from both short ends of the strip; this is where the sewing will begin and end on the zipper sides.

3. Referring to Diagram P, sew each side of the zipper to the fabric, backstitching at the 1½" marks.

4. On the wrong side of the fleece, carefully cut a straight line just between the stitching lines at each end of the zipper. See Diagram Q. Slip the ends of the zipper

through the openings. On the right side of the fleece, sew across the ends of the zipper, attaching the zipper to the fabric. Sew back and forth in a straight line, or stitch a triangle as shown in Diagram R. If you wish to add a tab to open and close the zipper, fold a 2" piece of ribbon in half and insert it between the fleece and the zipper before sewing. On the wrong side of the fabric, cut off the excess length on each end of the zipper.

5. Press the back and front of the fabric strip with the zipper attached. Then trim away the fleece from the underside of the zipper.

6. Mark the centers of all edges on the center strip and on the bag. With wrong sides together, pin the bag to the center strip, matching the marks on the edges. If you wish to add a handle to the bag, cut a 4" piece of ribbon and pin it to the bag edges as shown in Diagram S.

7. Sew around the bag edges with a ½" seam allowance. Reinforce the stitching on the ribbon handle. Trim the seam allowance with pinking shears, cutting slowly and carefully, and over a wastebasket.

8. To add a zipper pull, cut a strip of narrow ribbon or Ultrasuede. Thread it through the opening on the end of the zipper head, and tie in place. This will make the zipper easier to open and close.

9. Attach the monograms by hand or machine, referring to the photograph for placement.

LARGE BAG

MATERIALS

- ¾ yard of 60"-wide polar fleece
- 1 yard of 44"-wide mosquito netting
- 4 yards of 2"-wide flat cotton braid for handles
- 7" sports/outerwear zipper
- Thread to match

CUTTING

1. From the fleece, cut two 22" x 24" pieces. From the mosquito netting, cut two 22" x 24" pieces.
2. From the cotton braid, cut two 60"-long pieces and two 10"-long pieces.

ASSEMBLY

1. On a flat surface, place the zipper between the two 10" pieces of cotton braid, and pin. Make sure the braid pieces are aligned at the ends, and that the zipper is centered lengthwise between them. Topstitch the braid pieces to the zipper to make a zipper frame for the pocket. See Diagram T.
2. Layer each fleece piece with a netting piece for lining. Serge or machine baste around all outer edges to secure the two layers. The netting adds stability to the bag and keeps the fleece from stretching.
3. On one fleece piece, position the zipper frame so it is 7" from the top edge, and centered from side to side. Topstitch along the top and bottom edges of the braid, close to the edge and again ¼" away, as shown.
4. Position the 60" braid handles on each fleece piece so they are 5" in from each side and the raw ends are even with the bottom of the bag. The handles should cover the raw edges of the pocket frame. Pin the handles in place. See Diagram U.

5. Topstitch the braid to the fleece starting at the bottom raw edges. Stop stitching 2" from the top of the bag, pivot, and stitch across to the other edge of the braid. Pivot again and stitch to the bottom of the bag, referring again to Diagram U.
6. To finish the pocket, open the zipper. On the wrong side of the bag, cut away the fleece and the netting inside the stitching lines around the edge of the zipper frame.
7. Cut two pieces of fleece the width of the zipper frame and 6" to 10" long, depending on how large a pocket you want. Cut one piece of mosquito netting the same size. Layer the pieces wrong sides together, with the netting between the two pieces of fleece. Serge or overcast stitch around all edges.
8. Pin the pocket inside the bag over the zipper opening. Stitch the pocket in place on the bag. You may find it easier to stitch from the right side of the bag, so you can stitch directly over the previous topstitching.
9. With right sides together, stitch bag sections together on sides and bottom. To form a rectangular bottom, pin each side seam to the center fold line of the bag's bottom edge. Sew a 4" long seam across the triangular shape formed by the fold on each side of the bag. Turn right side out.
10. To hem, fold under 1" on the top edge of each fleece bag piece, then fold 1" again. Topstitch the hem in place.
11. Stuff your large tote with the other handy travel totes, and you're set to go anywhere!

DIAGRAM T

DIAGRAM U

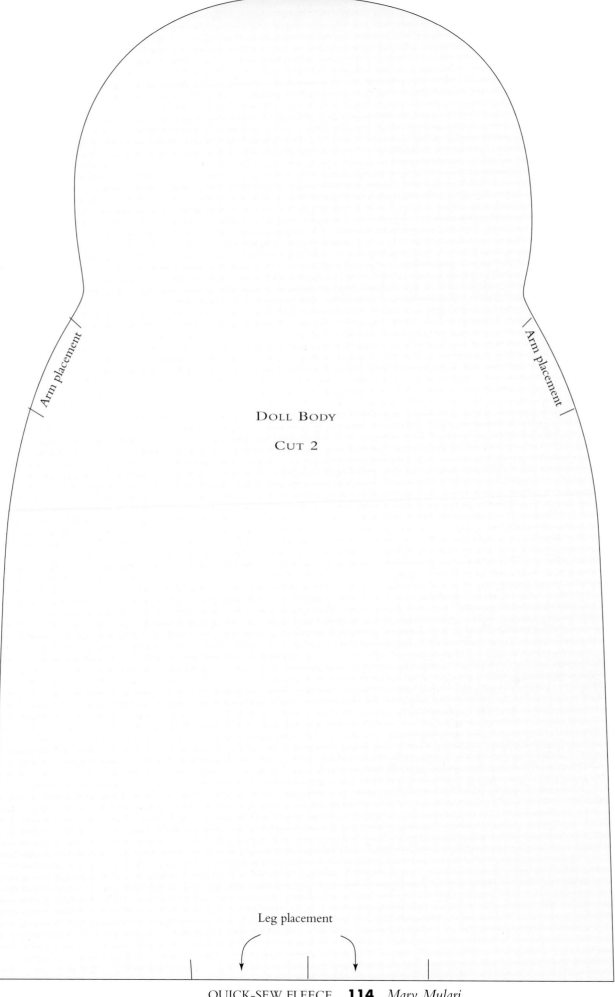

Arm placement

Arm placement

DOLL BODY

CUT 2

Leg placement

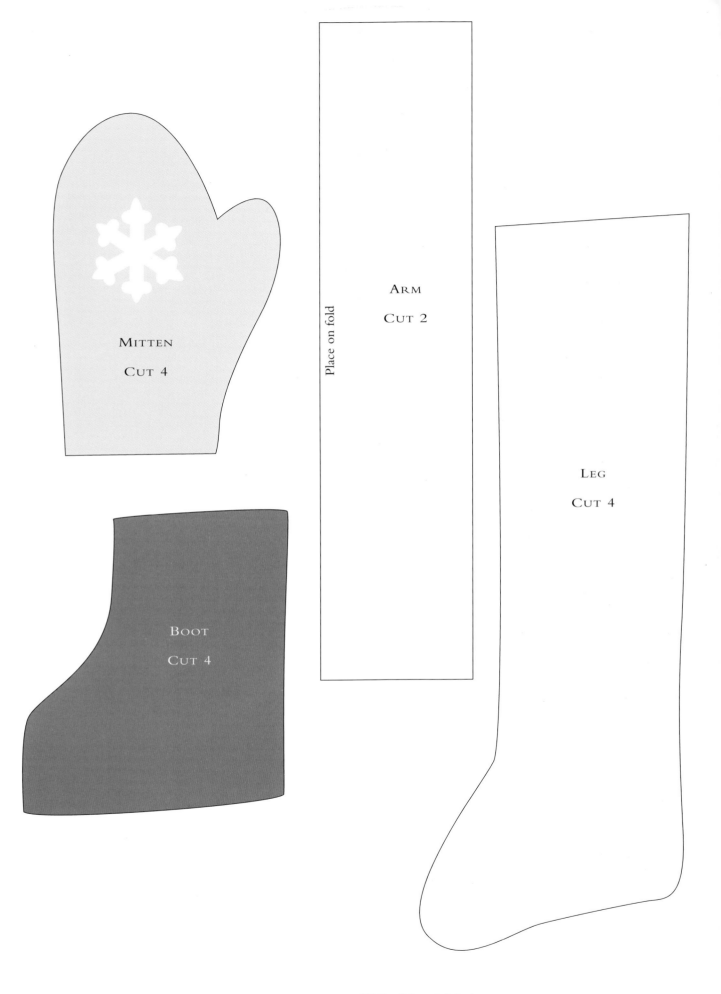

MITTEN

CUT 4

ARM

CUT 2

Place on fold

LEG

CUT 4

BOOT

CUT 4

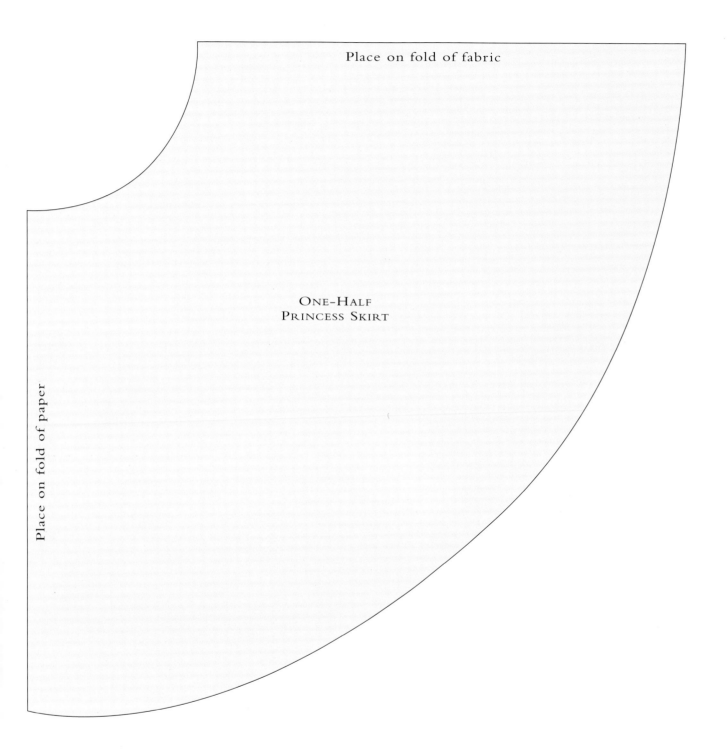

Place on fold of fabric

Place on fold of paper

ONE-HALF
PRINCESS SKIRT

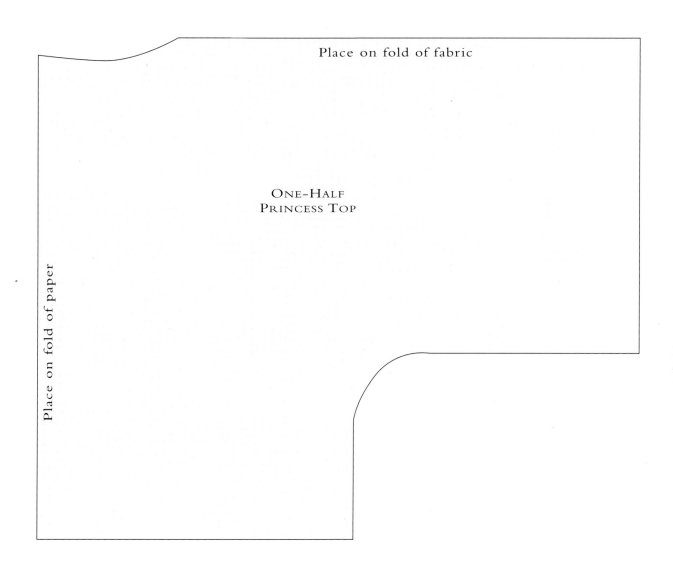

Place on fold of fabric

Place on fold of paper

ONE-HALF
PRINCESS TOP

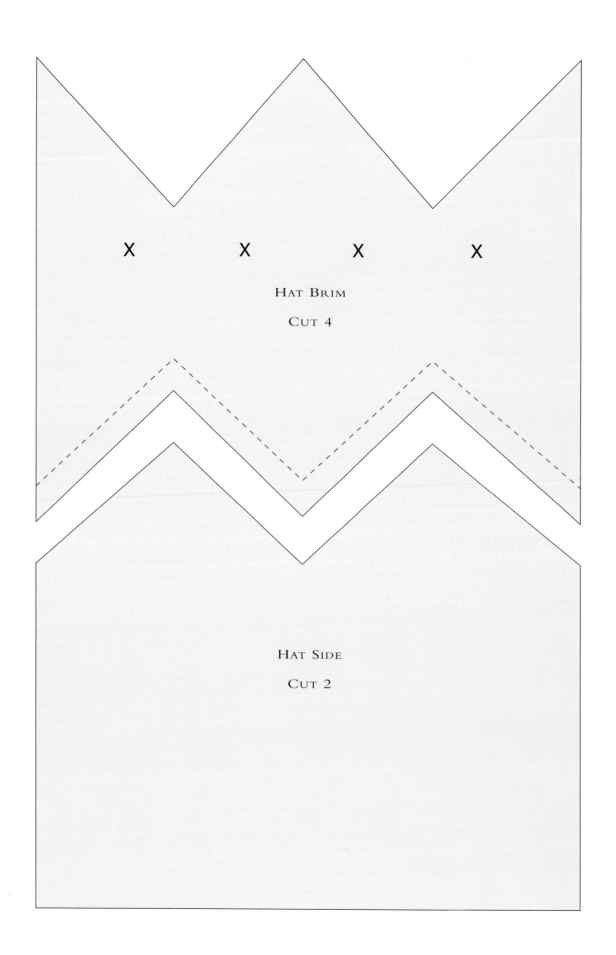

X X X X

HAT BRIM

CUT 4

HAT SIDE

CUT 2

HAT FRONT/BACK

CUT 2

Place on fold

HALF–CIRCLE
BAG

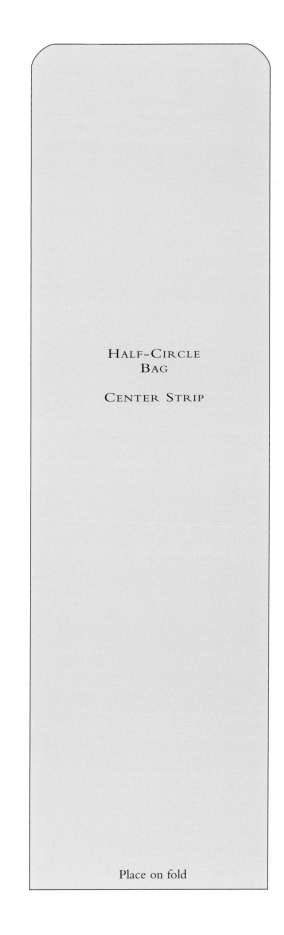

HALF-CIRCLE
BAG

CENTER STRIP

Place on fold

GENERAL INSTRUCTIONS

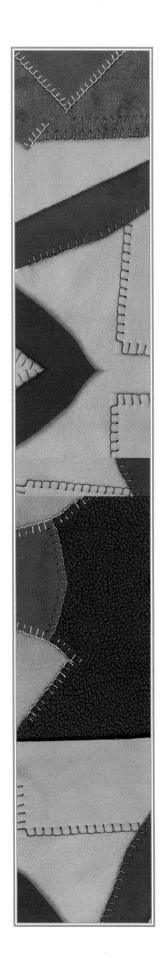

Working with fleece is fun, as long as you're familiar with a few basics about this exciting new fabric. Once you understand the properties of fleece—it is lightweight yet has loft and nap, it comes in a variety of styles and weights, and it's a stretch knit—you'll be ready to whip up any of the wonderful fashion, home accessories, or gift items in this book.

FOR EVERY PROJECT

As you gather your materials and supplies and begin each project, here are some guidelines you may find helpful:

- The fabric called for in the materials list is fleece, which is generally 60" wide.
- Fleece comes in various weights, including 100, 200, and 300; the higher the number, the thicker the loft. Other types of fabrics called for include Berber and Sherpa, which have a pile on the right side of the fabric.
- Materials lists include the type and color of fleece used. Feel free to use the style of fleece you prefer in your favorite colors.
- Seam allowances may vary by project. Some call for ¼" while others call for ½". For projects that use a purchased pattern, use the seam allowance specified in the pattern directions.
- Do not press seam allowances with an iron. Finger press only; an iron may melt the fabric.

WHICH SIDE IS THE RIGHT SIDE?

- Check to see if one side of the double-sided fleece is thicker than the other. The lower loft side is usually the right side.
- Does the fleece have a printed pattern? The side with the sharper image is the right side.
- Berber and Sherpa fleeces have a definite right side—the side with the thicker, curly nap.
- If all else fails, chose the side you like best and stick with it! Mark all wrong sides with a safety pin until the garment is completed.

FLEECE CARE

- Fleece doesn't shrink or bleed color, so there's no need to prewash.
- Cut out patterns using the "with nap" layout (Diagram A). Fleece has a nap, and cutting pieces in different directions will cause the garment to have different shading from one piece to another.
- To reduce pilling when laundering a finished garment, turn inside out and wash separately or with like garments using a powdered detergent.
- Dry on a low setting. Do not overdry.
- Don't use fabric softeners, as they tend to diminish the water-repellent feature of fleece.

PURCHASING A GARMENT PATTERN

Some projects call for a purchased garment pattern. Use these guidelines for selecting style and fit when working with fleece:

- Buy your typical size pattern, unless otherwise directed in the project directions.

- Simple, loose-fitting patterns work best for fleece, rather than ones with lots of specialized details, many seams, or sleeve caps that need to be eased to fit.

- Some of the garment projects call for adjustments to the original pattern. To save the original pattern for future use, trace the pattern as called for in the project directions onto pattern tracing material, such as Do-Sew.

NEEDLES, THREADS, AND PRESSER FEET

- Use good-quality polyester thread to match the fabric. Avoid bargain brands.

- Fleece is a knitted fabric, so use a Universal, Stretch, or Ballpoint needle. Select the needle size based on the weight of your fabric: 70/10 or 75/11 for lightweight fleece, 80/12 or 90/14 for midweight, and 100/16 for heavyweight fleece.

- Use your machine's standard presser foot or, to help avoid shifting layers, use a walking foot or roller foot.

SEWING BASICS FOR FLEECE

- Use as long a stitch length as possible. Try 7 or 9 stitches per inch (3mm-3.5mm). If stitch length is too short, you may stretch the fleece out of shape.

- If the garment is close-fitting, you may need to use a tighter stitch length so that the seams can give with wear. Try shortening to 12-14 stitches per inch (2mm- 2.5mm).

- If you are using a serger, use a three/four thread serger seam. Strengthen a three-thread serger seam with a straight stitch seam on a conventional sewing machine.

- If your serger has a differential feed option, you may need to adjust the feed to 1 or 1.5 for fleece with more stretch.

- If possible, sew with a standard ⅝" seam and trim to ⅜" or ¼".

- Edges can be serged, overcast, pinked, or left unfinished. If you plan to leave edges unfinished, it is best to trim them to ¼" to reduce the bulk of curling seam allowances (Diagram B).

- Another way to finish the seams is to leave seam allowances at ⅝" and double topstitch on the right side of the fabric. Stitch ¼" on each side of the seam, as shown in Diagram C. This provides a nice stitch detail on the right side and tames curling seam allowances.

BUTTONHOLES

- Use a stabilizer, such as Solvy by Sulky, to help prevent stretching. Draw the buttonhole length right on the stabilizer, pin or adhere in place, and stitch through the stabilizer (Diagram D). Be sure to use a permanent marker or disappearing ink marker to mark the buttonhole, or the ink could bleed when you rinse away the stabilizer.

- Since fleece garments usually don't call for an interfacing, use a tear-away stabilizer underneath the fabric layers for added support when stitching a buttonhole .

- Whenever possible, stitch buttonholes lengthwise since the stretch will be less than if you stitch on the crosswise grain.

- Use an open zigzag stitch rather than a tight satin stitch for buttonholes (Diagram E). A tight stitch might result in wavy edges when the buttonhole is cut open. Adjust your machine's preset stitch length to avoid this potential problem.

- When all else fails, take a clue from ready-to-wear fleece garments—install a zipper instead of buttons!

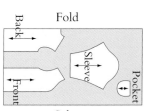

DIAGRAM A

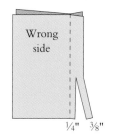

DIAGRAM B

DIAGRAM C

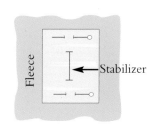

DIAGRAM D

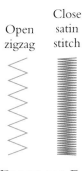

DIAGRAM E

SOURCES

KARI PEARSON
K. P. Kids & Company
Designing fun fabrics and fashions for kids won awards for Kari Pearson and her talented staff for their exhibit at a recent International Quilt Market. The patterns for the basic dress and vest are from her *Blooming Baby Boutique,* #1014. Kari's Fabrics are from South Seas Imports. Patterns for the Poseable Wooden Dolls are also available. For information or catalog, send $2 to: K. P. Kids, Rt. 1 Box 13, Fairfield, WA 99012; 509/291-6060.

MARGARET SINDELAR
Cottonwood Classics
Margaret creatively adapted McCall's Pattern #9019 for the Serged Jacket and Butterick #3925, View D, for the Tote Bag. The pillow form and batting are from Morning Glory Products (800/234-9105). Button trims for the Panda Pal outfits are from JHB International (303/751-8100). Margaret used the Viking #1+ Sewing Machine (800/446-2333). She can be contacted at: Cottonwood Classics, 4813 Cody Drive, West Des Moines, IA 50265; 515/225-8409.

CHERYL JUKICH
Threadbare Pattern Company
The projects Cheryl created for this collection are just a sampling of her talents as a fabric artisan. The double-sided (flannel on one side and fleece on the other) fabric for the Fireside Pillow is Polar Fleece® and widely available in fabric stores. Cheryl's extensive line includes an interchangeable embellished vest series and the Quick-Quilt ™ collection, which features a technique for turning a humble sweatshirt into a quilted garment using no batting or lining. For more information contact: Threadbare Pattern Company, Department QSQ3, P.O. Box 1484, Havelock, NC 28532; 800/4-Pattern (800/472-8837).

JANET CARIJA BRANDT
Carijarts
For her clever Shades of Autumn rug, Janet used rug warp available from Cushing & Company (800/626-7847). Janet has several best-selling books to her credit. For more information, contact her at: 2136 Silver Lane Drive, Indianapolis, IN 46203; 317/352-0059.

NANCY CORNWELL
Stretch & Sew® Fabrics
In addition to designing unique clothing and decorative accessories, Nancy enjoys traveling and teaching, sharing her techniques with others. Nancy used Stretch & Sew® Fabrics Patterns: #375 for the Berber Pullover, #303 for the Crossover Vest, and #1083 for the Cardigan. For mail order information for an extensive line of patterns, fabrics, and supplies, contact Stretch & Sew® Fabrics, Dept. AP, 19725 40th Ave. West Suite G, Lynnwood, WA 98036; 425/776-3700.

MERRY NADER
Merry Nader's Designs
Merry is well-known in needlework circles for her charming and intricately-detailed embroidery. Merry has creatively adapted her embroidery to fleece using DMC perle cotton and the Caron Collection of watercolors. For more information, contact Merry at: P.O. Box 1870, Royal Oak, MI 48068-1870; 248/548-2715.

JUDITH CARTER & LEIGH ANNE ROACH
Custom Threads
The pillow form, fiberfill, and poly pellets used in projects are from Fairfield Processing Corporation, widely available in fabric and craft stores. Embroidery floss and Zweigart canvas were supplied by The Needlepoint Place (800/979-3570). This talented design duo combine years of creative experience in the design and needlework field. For information about their creative services company, contact them at: Custom Threads, P.O. Box 660612, Birmingham, AL 35266-0612; 205/822-6660.

JANIS BULLIS
Creative Services
Janis has contributed to numerous publications and brings a wealth of experience to the sewing and needlework industry. The Ethnic Vest was created from McCall's Pattern #8699. For more information, contact Janis at: Creative Services, 20 Shuit Place, Central Valley, NY 10917; 914/928-2170.

MARY MULARI
Mary's Productions
With numerous best-selling sewing books to her credit, traveling and teaching is almost a way of life for Mary. For information on her books and teaching schedule, Mary can be contacted at: Mary's Productions, Box 87, 219 North Main, Aurora, MN 55705; 218/229-2804.

PROJECT INDEX

SELECTED PUBLICATIONS FROM MARTINGALE & CO.

QUILT DESIGN

All New! Copy Art for Quilters illustrated by Barb Tourtillotte
Color: The Quilter's Guide by Christine Barnes
Design Essentials: The Quilter's Guide by Lorraine Torrence
Design Your Own Quilts by Judy Hopkins
*Fine Art Quilts: Work by Artists of the Contemporary Quilt
    Art Association*
Freedom in Design by Mia Rozmyn
The Log Cabin Design Workbook by Christal Carter
The Nature of Design by Joan Colvin
QuiltSkills: Workshops from the Quilters' Guild Australia
Surprising Designs from Traditional Quilt Blocks by Carole M. Fure
Whimsies & Whynots by Mary Lou Weidman

FINISHING TECHNIQUES

Borders by Design by Paulette Peters
The Border Workbook by Janet Kime
A Fine Finish by Cody Mazuran
Happy Endings by Mimi Dietrich
Interlacing Borders by Donna Hussain
Loving Stitches by Jeana Kimball
Press for Success by Myrna Giesbrecht
Quilting Design Sourcebook by Dorothy Osler
Quilting Makes the Quilt by Lee Cleland
Sensational Settings by Joan Hanson
Traditional Quilts with Painless Borders by Sally Schneider
    and Barbara J. Eikmeier
The Ultimate Book of Quilt Labels by Margo J. Clabo

FOUNDATION/PAPER PIECING

Classic Quilts with Precise Foundation Piecing by Tricia Lund
    and Judy Pollard
Crazy but Pieceable by Hollie A. Milne
Easy Machine Paper Piecing by Carol Doak
Easy Mix & Match Machine Paper Piecing by Carol Doak
Easy Paper-Pieced Keepsake Quilts by Carol Doak
Easy Paper-Pieced Miniatures by Carol Doak
Easy Reversible Vests by Carol Doak
Go Wild with Quilts by Margaret Rolfe
Go Wild with Quilts—Again! by Margaret Rolfe
A Quilter's Ark by Margaret Rolfe
Show Me How to Paper Piece by Carol Doak

HOME DECORATING

Decorate with Quilts & Collections by Nancy J. Martin
The Home Decorator's Stamping Book by Linda Barker
Living with Little Quilts by Alice Berg, Mary Ellen Von Holt,
    and Sylvia Johnson
Make Room for Quilts by Nancy J. Martin
Soft Furnishings for Your Home by Sharyn Skrabanich
Welcome Home: Debbie Mumm

MACHINE QUILTING/SEWING

Machine Needlelace and Other Embellishment Techniques
    by Judy Simmons
Machine Quilting Made Easy by Maurine Noble
Machine Quilting with Decorative Threads by Maurine Noble
    and Elizabeth Hendricks
Thread Magic by Ellen Anne Eddy
Threadplay with Libby Lehman

ROTARY CUTTING/SPEED PIECING

A New Slant on Bargello Quilts by Marge Edie
Around the Block with Judy Hopkins
All-Star Sampler by Roxanne Carter
Bargello Quilts by Marge Edie
Basic Quiltmaking Techniques for Strip Piecing by Paulette Peters
Blockbender Quilts by Margaret J. Miller
Block by Block by Beth Donaldson
Class-Act Quilts
Down the Rotary Road with Judy Hopkins
Easy Seasonal Wall Quilts by Deborah J. Moffett-Hall
Easy Star Sampler by Roxanne Carter
The Joy of Quilting by Joan Hanson and Mary Hickey
Lively Little Logs by Donna Fite McConnell
Magic Base Blocks for Unlimited Quilt Designs by Patty Barney
    and Cooky Schock
Mirror Manipulations by Gail Valentine
More Quilts for Baby by Ursula Reikes
More Strip-Pieced Watercolor Magic by Deanna Spingola
Patchwork Pantry by Suzette Halferty and Carol C. Porter
A Perfect Match by Donna Lynn Thomas
Quilting Up a Storm by Lydia Quigley
Quilts for Baby by Ursula Reikes
Rotary Riot by Judy Hopkins and Nancy J. Martin
Rotary Roundup by Judy Hopkins and Nancy J. Martin
Shortcuts by Donna Lynn Thomas
Simply Scrappy Quilts by Nancy J. Martin
Square Dance by Martha Thompson
Start with Squares by Martha Thompson
Strip-Pieced Watercolor Magic by Deanna Spingola
Stripples by Donna Lynn Thomas
Stripples Strikes Again! by Donna Lynn Thomas
Strips that Sizzle by Margaret J. Miller
Two-Color Quilts by Nancy J. Martin

STITCHERY/NEEDLE ARTS

Christmas Ribbonry by Camela Nitschke
Hand-Stitched Samplers from I Done My Best by Saundra White
Miniature Baltimore Album Quilts by Jenifer Buechel
A Passion for Ribbonry by Camela Nitschke
A Silk-Ribbon Album by Jenifer Buechel
Victorian Elegance by Lezette Thomason

SURFACE DESIGN/FABRIC MANIPULATION

15 Beads: A Guide to Creating One-of-a-Kind Beads
    by Jane Dunnewold
The Art of Handmade Paper and Collage by Cheryl Stevenson
Complex Cloth by Jane Dunnewold
Dyes & Paints: A Hands-On Guide to Coloring Fabric by Elin Noble
Hand-Dyed Fabric Made Easy by Adriene Buffington

Many of these books are available through your local fabric, quilt, or craft shop.
For more information, call, write, fax, or e-mail for our free full-color catalog.

Martingale & Company
Toll-free: 1-800-426-3126
International: 1-425-483-3313
24-Hour Fax: 1-425-486-7596
PO Box 118
Bothell, WA 98041-0118 USA
Web site: www.patchwork.com
E-mail: info@patchwork.com